MONSTER
Shallow-Water
STRIPERS

T0303000

8 99852 00109 5

MONSTER
Shallow-Water
STRIPERS

How to Catch the Largest
Bass of Your Life

CAPT. JIM WHITE

HEADWATER
BOOKS

Monster Shallow-Water Stripers:
How to Catch the Largest Bass of Your Life
Capt. Jim White

Copyright © 2009 by Headwater Books

Published by
HEADWATER BOOKS
531 Harding Street
New Cumberland, PA 17070
www.headwaterbooks.com

FIRST EDITION

10 9 8 7 6 5 4 3 2 1

ISBN: 978-0-9793460-9-5

Library Congress Catalog Number: 2008938125

Cover photo by Jim White
Illustrations by Dave Hall
Knot illustrations courtesy of Ande and Stackpole Books
Transducer illustrations courtesy of Lowrance
Cover design by Ryan Scheife, Mayfly Design
Book design and composition by John Reinhardt Book Design

Printed in the United States of America

This is the largest and most comprehensive book I've written, and I dedicate it to the most important people in my life.

First, to my father, Jim White, for introducing me to fishing when I was old enough to walk. Through him, I met some of the greatest surf fishermen of the golden era of surf casting. He passed away in 1992 at the age of eighty-three, but I often call on him to help me out when the fishing is tough. I know he's catching monster stripers in a better place; I just hope that he saves a few for me when we meet again.

Second, to my wife, Nancy, who has put up with me for the last thirty-one years. She's been there for me, has never complained about my passion for fishing, and has been my motivation and inspiration. She is by far the best catch I've ever made. I love her beyond words. She is not only my wife but my best friend as well.

I learned from my grandfather that there were only three things in life that no one can take away from you: your dignity, your self-respect, and your family name. If you gave up one or all, it was because you let it happen and not something someone did to you. I taught that to my kids, and they've made me proud of the way they have lived their lives. My son, Justin, who works with me in our business, has become a respected captain in his own right. My daughters, Melissa and Ashley, have grown to be exceptional women. I love them with all my heart.

Lastly, I dedicate this book to my grandchildren, Devon James White (D. J.) and Ava and Samantha Powers. They are now my life's purpose. D. J. has grown to be a skillful and knowledgeable angler at a very young age. He hunts, plays sports, and fishes like his family before him, with a love and passion for the sport. Ava and Samantha are the sweetest things that God has ever created. They are one bundle of joy. I love them with all my heart.

CONTENTS

ACKNOWLEDGMENTS

SO MANY PEOPLE NEED TO BE THANKED, I'm afraid I will forget or overlook someone. But, I'll do the best I can, and I apologize if I leave anyone out.

To Lefty Kreh, for his guidance, wealth of knowledge and wisdom, and unconditional friendship for all these years. There is truly no one like him. To Mike Laptew, my bizzaro friend who helps me keep my perspective when things get tough and is one of the most optimistic people I've ever known. To Nick Curcione, my *paison*, whose advice and friendship have been among the most valuable in my life and who is one of the funniest people I've ever met. To Shaw Grigsby, who is without doubt one of the most talented and experienced anglers I've ever had the opportunity to fish with.

To all the editors who published my writing over the years and believed what I wrote was interesting enough for others to read, even when they had to fix it. I will forever be grateful to Tim Coleman, former editor of *The Fisherman* magazine, Zack Harvey, former editor of *The Fisherman* magazine and *Center Console* magazine, and Mike Connor of *Shallow Water Angler*.

I was fortunate enough to have known, met, and fished with some of the greatest anglers that ever lived. Frank Woolner, Hal Lyman, Charlie Murat, Jerry Sylvester, Bob Pond, Art Lavallee Sr., and a host of others all shared their knowledge and wisdom with a young boy who was hungry to learn. I will always be grateful for what they taught me.

One more group of guys deserves more than just a brief mention, but space prohibits anything more. They say that only ten percent of the fishermen catch all the fish. Then there's that two or three percent who catch even more. They are the best of best and a sort of All-Star Fishing Society that never gets mentioned or given any credit for what they do or know. I learned a long time ago that there is always someone who is better, and these guys are in their own league. In Rhode Island they are well known. They seek no ink, no fame, no spotlight; they simply go out and catch fish where everyone else believes they don't exist. I've admired them for years and will always. They are the true anglers in every sense of the word. Some of them are close friends. Others I've only met a few times. I believe each of them will know who I'm speaking about without revealing names. I just want to say that they have my utmost respect, and I continually aspire to be one of them, although that will not likely happen.

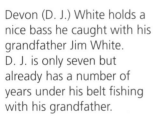

Devon (D. J.) White holds a nice bass he caught with his grandfather Jim White. D. J. is only seven but already has a number of years under his belt fishing with his grandfather.

INTRODUCTION

THIS BOOK IS A CULMINATION of more than forty years of fishing for striped bass. Information on fishing in shallow water has lagged behind most other aspects of fishing for big stripers. In many cases, an awful lot of anglers simply don't believe that catching stripers in water as shallow as two or three feet is possible. The perception is that you always have to fish the deepest water. I watch this contingent of nonbelievers speed past me almost daily.

For many years I fished the same way most everyone else did. I'd head for the offshore reefs, islands, and other commonly targeted big-fish haunts. In time, I got tired of going so far and taking so long to begin fishing that I started fishing closer to home. It was partly the challenge that lured me and my friends to shallower waters, and partly because fishing closer to home gave us more time to fish and enjoy being out on the water. Never having to travel more than ten or fifteen minutes to begin fishing seemed to have a lot of advantages, even if the fish weren't so big. But I eventually learned that there was also a wide array of opportunities to catch big fish in these overlooked areas.

When I decided to open a guide business in 1990, I wanted to be different than almost everyone else. There were already a lot of charter operations fishing for stripers at Block Island, Fisher's Island, Cutty-hunk, the Vineyard, and other traditional offshore areas. I'd had my

Capt. Jim White hauls in a 35-pound striper on a big bunker fly at night. Many anglers avoid fly fishing at night because it has its own set of challenges.

fill of long runs, big seas, rocking and rolling all day long, and fighting the wind on the way home. It just didn't excite me any longer, and I suspected that there was a large, untapped body of anglers out there who also preferred not to fish in such conditions.

I then looked to Narragansett Bay, which I had fished since I was a small boy, and saw absolutely no one there, except one friend who I'd known for over thirty years. I decided that I would concentrate my efforts there. I already had a lot of time invested in the bay. Aside from experience there as a boy, I'd caught thousands of pounds of big stripers there when I fished commercially in the 1970s. I say pounds of fish because that's how they were measured in those days.

So, backed by the years of knowledge I already possessed, I decided to begin right back where I had started when I'd accompanied my dad and grandfather on fishing trips. I knew that it would take an awful lot of work to catch a big fish out of a fishery that was absolutely crammed with small fish. Why was it crammed with small fish? Once the commercial net season was allowed to come back in 1992 on a limited basis, and then pretty much full-blown in 1995, the sizes of the fish began to drop dramatically. What had taken only a few hours of fishing to catch now took all night or even several days. Once that leveled off in the mid to late 1990s most of the fish that were available were small. A 6- or 8-pound fish was picture-worthy. To find the largest fish, I probed, studied, recorded, and fished every square inch of water that I knew of and investigated many more. As time went by, I began catching fish in the teens to the mid-20-pound range on fly rods, and definite patterns began to emerge.

Many of the fish in the beginning years were small school bass like this one. There weren't many "keepers" then. Not all fish can be or will be monsters. This schoolie bass decided to eat a big 7½-inch Slug-Go for his breakfast. Even small fish will take large lures and flies.

As this part of my guide business began to grow, I began getting customers from all over the country as well from Europe. Then, the bigger names in fly fishing began inquiring about our unique fishery—names like Popovics, Curcione, Blanton, Clouser, and even the master himself, Lefty Kreh. All wanted to pursue these creatures in shallow water, and all looked for the opportunity to tangle with huge stripers on fly rods. Back when our business was focused primarily on fly fishing, our biggest fly-rod striper was just over 39 pounds. Not too shabby for a fishery overrun with 16- to 24-inch fish. But we were still learning.

As the years passed and our fishery began to change, we changed with it. Perhaps because of the advances in tackle or some of the inherent difficulties in learning how to fly cast, our clients now were more light-tackle oriented. This led to more change, more challenges, more

In time we started to catch fish in the high teens to low twenties. There were not a lot of large fish, however, and it took a lot of work and time on the water to catch them.

time working on new techniques, and still more time evolving our business to meet the current influx of highly motivated light-tackle anglers. This shift opened up a whole new dimension to finding bigger and bigger fish, as well as to the areas we could now target with light tackle.

Today our guide business focuses on landing fish from 20 pounds or more in shallow water on light tackle as well as on fly rods. In the spring of 2007 we put our first 60-pound striper in the boat, a milestone that we've worked hard on for eighteen years now. During that same year, we also lost one at the boat when the hook flew out of the beast's mouth and landed between my thumb and index finger. We estimated that fish to weigh 60 pounds or more.

Since 1990, which is eighteen years at the time of writing, our two boats have landed 18,859 striped bass. That's an average of 1,100 striped bass per season. During my fishing career as a guide, I've land-

After wading the grassy shoreline and tossing a big fly parallel to this grass and rock structure, Capt. Jim White landed this 30-pound striper. He gets ready to release the fish back into the shallow water it came from.

ed or helped anglers land 1 fish of 60 pounds, 14 fish between 50 and 58 pounds, 216 fish between 40 and 49 pounds, and 336 fish between 30 and 39 pounds.

The final tally for the 2007 season was impressive—our best season so far for big shallow-water stripers. We caught 1 fish over 60 pounds, 4 fish over 50 pounds, 16 fish over 40 pounds, 42 fish over 30 pounds, and 123 fish over 20 pounds.

The time, effort, and knowledge gained through tens of thousands of hours on the water had paid big dividends. Hopefully, that success will continue well into the future as we learn and gain more knowledge while fishing. And this emphasizes a central theme of this book. Nothing substitutes for time and experience on the water. There is no such thing as a successful angler who only fishes on Saturday mornings. Another point is that absolutely no one gets to know it all or gets to decipher all the answers to the fishing puzzle. Fishing for striped bass is a constant and neverending learning process. Once you accept

To catch large bass, you need to target them, which often means passing up opportunities to catch a lot of smaller fish. The best anglers, such as Bill Nolan (above), spend lots of time on the water and challenge conventional thinking.

that fact, you will not only learn more but probably catch more fish as well. Learn to accept new ideas and challenges and don't readily accept old wives' tales as fact. Challenge yourself as well as almost any given idea of how large striped bass are supposed to be caught. You may find yourself opening up new doors and new opportunities you never thought were possible.

CHAPTER 1

FEEDING STATIONS

L IKE MANY OTHER GAMEFISH, stripers instinctively search out areas that they have learned to use to their advantage when it comes time to put on the feed bag. Such feeding stations, as they are called, are areas where you are likely to find stripers feeding as well as resting throughout the season. I have caught fish in all these areas over the years. Some are better than others, but all have their own little secrets to fishing them successfully. What follows is a brief description of each type of station and what I have learned about them. Flats, rivers, and points get their own chapters in this book, but all of the feeding stations in this chapter are capable of producing fish from 20 to well over 50 pounds when the conditions are right.

It is important to understand that big fish don't feed every day or during every tide for days or weeks on end. The times that they are active and available to those fishing in shallow water are limited. Learn to fish the peak times for the most success. Look for those conditions that will lead big stripers into the shallows to feed: at night, during or just after a storm, during rising water at dawn or dusk, or during the right moon phases. If you add up all the days of a season during

High rocky cliffs with rocky structure beneath them usually have white water from waves pushing against them. Stripers like to feed here and will take lures and flies fished in tight in the whitewater wash.

which big fish are likely to be active, they might amount to three weeks. The key is to concentrate your efforts during the best times. Small fish can be caught on a fairly regular basis by almost anyone; big fish are taken by those who study the habits and movements of big fish. A bass of 20 pounds or more has already beaten the odds in the ocean. He's dodged nets, traps, boaters, surf casters, and many more obstacles to reach that size.

Whether you are fishing a big river, a huge flat, a large cove, or an expansive bay, the size of the area where most of the fish are going to be found will be extremely small. The areas where huge stripers tend to gather and feed will be even smaller still. The more unproductive feeding areas you can eliminate, the better your chances of success. Also, bigger fish seem to gravitate to the same areas. Once you discover big fish in an area, check it often.

Sandbars

Stripers like to be next to the deepest water available. This provides them with a quick avenue of escape if and when danger arises, and it also gives them a safe travel lane both to and from the bar under most tidal conditions.

Many sandbars are just humps of sand that have been stacked up by wind and tide and have little or no deeper water nearby. Sandbars like this will only hold fish for short periods of time and will hardly ever attract fish over 10 or 15 pounds. Larger fish require deep water close by; the closer, the better.

Bars adjacent to channels, deep holes, drop-offs, and other bottom features will likely hold more and bigger fish for longer periods of time. The deeper water allows the bigger fish to stay longer in the shallower water and feed. Some sandbars can go from 2 to 3 feet of water

Jerry Gibbs fishing a Slug-Go off a rocky shoreline point on a cloudy, overcast day. These types of days can offer some of the best fishing of the year. *Mike Laptew photo*

Sandbars offer striped bass a place to feed and also break the current, causing baitfish to become disoriented. Stripers will often hang in the deeper water at A, B, C, or D to feed.

right down to 20 feet in a matter of only a few feet. This quick change in depth also causes rips that help push the baitfish up and over the top of the bar and into deeper water where big fish lie in wait.

Almost all predatory fish will lie facing into the current waiting for the food to be swept by to them. The larger the fish, the more likely this is to be true, since they will expend as little energy as possible to get their food. They have already learned from years of survival what works best and what doesn't. Big, old fish are lazy by nature. If I race with my grandson, who is now seven, he's going to get to the finish line long before I do, since I'm pushing sixty years old. Fish are no different than people when it comes to expending energy. The younger, faster ones get to the food long before the older, tired, and lazy fish do. Bigger fish will normally set themselves up on the opposite side of the tidal flow. For example, when the current is flowing from right to left, stripers will be facing the bar on the left-hand side waiting for the

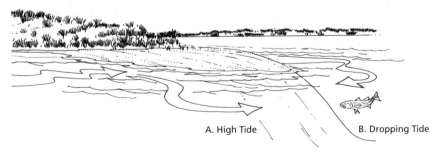

A. High Tide　　　　　　　B. Dropping Tide

Stripers often hunt on or near where the bar meets deep water. This provides them with a quick avenue of escape if and when danger arises, and it also gives them a safe travel lane both to and from the bar under most tidal conditions.

Big stripers are available even during the day, provided you are fishing in the right areas. Knowing where the fish are likely to be takes time on the water.

baitfish to be swept to them so that they use as little energy as possible when feeding.

Whether wading or fishing from a boat, position yourself down-current so that you face in the direction that the fish are going to be moving. Then present your lure or fly up-current so that it comes back toward you. For example, if the current or tide is running south to north, cast your lure or fly to the south, up into the current and tide. Too many anglers go to an area and begin casting helter-skelter without thinking about what the fish are looking for or exactly how and where they have placed themselves for an easy meal. Leaving the boat is not as popular in the Northeast as it is in Florida where flats fishing has evolved into a science. But accessing

> Big fish will usually be found in pairs or groups of four to six fish.

When rips form, fish will hold in the seam between the calm and ripply water and wait for bait, disoriented by the turbulent water, to be swept to them.

a sandbar by boat and then wading to fish it is an effective technique, especially if the bar is far from shore.

Sandbars and points of land are usually best when the water flow is at its strongest and the wind is against the tide, causing the dropping water and the wind-blown surface water to collide. Make sure that you fish all sides of the bar or point before you leave. Even water that doesn't look like it will hold fish can be full of stripers. Look for any holes, rocks, weed beds, and drop-offs where fish may congregate and hold. Start at the outside edges and slowly work your way into either side of the bar.

Rips and eddies are common around sandbars. Rips form when the currents meet an obstruction such as a bar or rocks. The turbulent water is usually noticeable. Points will usually have eddies on the back side of them where the water tends to swirl in a circular motion. In many areas these conditions will only last for a short time. Rips and eddies can form one right after another in some bay systems, allowing you to fish one or more in succession. But you have to know where they are and when they will form, which takes a lot of time on the water so that you can record these events. The closer the bar is to deep water, the more pronounced and dramatic the rip and eddy will be. On any given day, the type of current movement that you are looking for will only develop on certain stages of the tide, and in some cases only for a short period of time.

Rips, no matter what creates them, can provide great fishing. In 2007 Billy Nolan and I did a television shoot with *On the Water* magazine. The morning of the shoot, the current just wasn't moving. I said to Billy, "We need to find some moving water or we aren't going to catch much of anything."

As we drifted along, I notice this point jutting out from a bulkhead, which was part of an old pier that once stood there. The wind had picked up, and a small rip line was forming at the end of it. We moved to it and threw our live menhaden right up against the point and into the small rip. Over the next 30 minutes we landed 16 fish up to 30 pounds from an area no bigger than your living room.

Coves and Bays

Coves and bays have an awful lot of different feeding stations within them. The first thing to do if you are targeting big fish is to eliminate from your search the nonproductive areas that only attract smaller fish or no fish at all.

Grass beds along the shoreline often concentrate bait trying to hide

Rocky structure along the shoreline usually indicates similar structure below the surface. The presence of gulls usually mean the presence of baitfish, and some nice stripers lurking about.

Grass lines like this are natural areas for baitfish to congregate. They will usually go into the grass on high tide and then get flushed out when the tide begins to drop. Check these areas on a falling tide for some exciting fishing.

from predators in the high water. Smaller stripers will usually chase the bait right to the edge of the grass and sometimes right inside it. Bigger fish will almost always hold at the first drop away from the shoreline and wait for the tide to flush the bait out of the grass and to them. Look for a slight to moderate drop in water depth between the shoreline grass and some deeper water. That is where the bigger fish will set up and patrol, waiting to feed. They won't expend all the energy the smaller fish do launching attacks into the grass. Being smarter in their feeding habits is how they got to be bigger.

Docks and Piers

Pro bass anglers fish for a lot of money, and they fish a lot of docks and piers. All big fish—regardless of whether they are striped bass, largemouth bass, bluefish, or pike—like structure. Stripers will often rest in the shade beneath a moored boat or underneath a pier or floating dock, waiting for the right conditions to feed, but they do so only for a

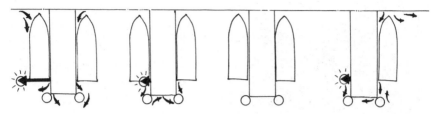

Piers and docks hold fish at certain times of the season, especially during the spring and fall of the year when the water is cool. Fish them early or late in the evening when the dock lights are on.

short time, ranging from just a few days to a couple of weeks depending on the availability of bait and the water temperature.

I know two anglers who have made an art and science out of fishing beneath boat docks and piers, and they have wrestled out some pretty impressive fish. They do it in the morning just before the sun comes up and after dark when no one is around. Their success speaks for itself.

Piers, docks, and bulkheads will hold big fish at certain times of the season. Many anglers overlook these areas, but they are excellent spots to find big stripers. You'll need heavier gear to fish this type of structure properly.

A nice striper that came from behind moored sailboats in a harbor. Sailboats provide shade from the sun as well as concentrating baitfish beneath them. If the harbor has some current, all the better.

Hundreds of boats leave that cove every day during the fishing season, unaware of how many fish they have just passed by.

Most anglers tend to avoid these types of areas, as they can be difficult to fish. Once you hook a good fish, the first thing it will do is head for the pilings, docks, and submerged junk usually lying on the bottom of most marinas, so you need to use heavy rods and leaders. Once a fish is hooked, you need to pressure him immediately and put the boots to him so he doesn't wrap you around dock lines or other structure.

You must also be able to cast your lure accurately so that you can fish beneath the docks and around the pilings. The best way to fish this type of structure is parallel to it, getting your lure or jig as close to the dock or pier as possible. A heavy jig with a plastic trailer is without a doubt the best lure for this job. It will get you down deep, and in some cases underneath the dock, where the fish are hiding.

Docks and piers are also best when fished under the cover of darkness. As most docks and piers in marinas are well lit, there will be dozens of shadow lines to fish. If you've ever been at a marina on a calm, windless night and paid close attention, you have probably heard the sound of fish busting water all over the place. On some mornings the fish are beneath my dock feeding when my clients show up. I never thought it would be a good idea to tell them that we were simply going to go to the outside end of the docks and fish there, but I've wanted to do just that on some days.

Rock Piles

Rock piles can be found in very shallow water or in depths of 20, 30, or even 60 feet. Along the shoreline or in relatively shallow water, they offer an easy reference point to begin fishing. As the water depth increases, they become a lot more difficult to find and to fish for many anglers. Rock piles may consist of one or two small rocks lying on an otherwise sandy bottom or a series of rocks the size of a house piled on and next to each other.

Rock piles away from the shoreline, surrounded by water on all sides, are the ones to target. Sometimes the bass can be found behind one in only inches of water, waiting for food to go by on the outside of the rock. Make sure you cast your lure or fly behind, to the sides of, and in front of any visible rocks because you never know where the fish are holding. Hitting the target is critical. Rocks that have some type of white-water wash coming off of them due to wave action are also good bets.

Fish rocks in deeper water with a sinking fly line and Clouser Deep Minnow or a deep-diving lure or plastic shad on a jighead. Probe all sides of the rock, including the front, and work the water column from

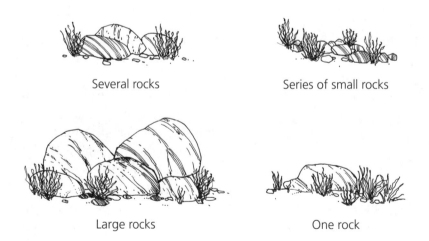

Several rocks

Series of small rocks

Large rocks

One rock

Stripers feed around rock piles, which is why they are known as rockfish in other areas of the country. Rock piles that have current and are close to deep water are the best.

Rock piles can be attached to the shoreline or away from the shoreline below the water. Shoreline rocks are the easiest to see. Use electronics to find those beneath the surface.

the top to the bottom to find where the fish are holding. Fish-holding locations can change on a daily basis, so it is best that you get in the habit of methodically fishing the entire area.

A series of rocks, either strung out in a line or in some other configuration, have openings that provide travel routes for fish. Sometimes, depending on the tide, fish only feed at or move through certain openings. Therefore, it is necessary to fish as many of the openings as possible. On high tides, when there is some water just covering the rocks, toss a popping plug or a fly-rod popper over the rocks, and work the area from one end to the other to help determine where the fish are holding.

> Large fish usually occupy the same areas year after year.

Bridges and Shadow Lines

Most rivers have a bridge or two going over them—some even more. Big bass will hide out behind the abutments to escape the strong flow of water coming down or going upriver. Abutment corners are excellent places to fish early and late in the day as the bass move up to the shallower parts of the abutments to feed.

In the morning and late afternoon, the low-angled sun will create a shadow line on the water. Stripers will hide in and ambush their prey from this shadow line during the day and during the night when the lights on the bridge cast a shadow on the water. Shadows conceal their presence, and our clients have taken many nice bass during the day.

Breachways

Breachways are man-made rock barriers that usually separate a tidal pond from the open ocean and are generally associated with barrier beaches. They are usually dug deeper than the surrounding area and are lined on each side with rocks to form a wall. They look like a small river channel from the ocean to the tidal pond in back. They help the salt pond exchange fresh salt water each day to keep its salinity high and to help flush the pond of sediments that build up. Over time, the breachway passage loses its effectiveness and needs to be cleaned out or re-dug to continue the natural exchange of water.

Bridges provide shadow lines during the day—and at night—and stripers will hold in the shadows when feeding in tidal rivers. Abutments break the flow of water and fish will hold on the down side of the current.

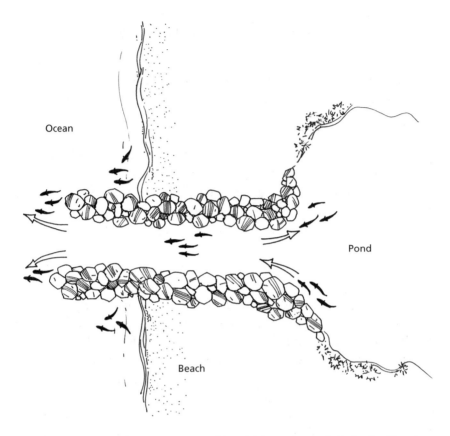

Breachways connect the open ocean with a tidal pond, usually in back of barrier beaches. The outside and inside corners, as well as the channel, will hold fish.

Breachways can provide excellent fishing. Baitfish are sucked out of the pond when the tide drops, and the big fish wait in front for the food to come to them. Two of the more famous breachways along the striper coast are the Charlestown and Weekapaug breachways in Charlestown, Rhode Island. Thousands of big fish have been taken from the end of each one as well as inside the breachways. When fishing a breachway, the normal tide range will usually change, sometimes by hours. For example, when the tide begins to drop on the ocean front, it is still rising inside the breachway and the pond in back.

Menhaden Schools

Feeding stations that attract big stripers don't necessarily have to be fixed objects beneath the water or attached to land. One of the best mobile feeding stations is a school of menhaden, also known as pogies or bunker. When this oily baitfish is plentiful, stripers come from miles around to feed on them. A school of menhaden will even draw stripers away from areas that they would normally be found.

Many people simply snag their bait out of the school, let it drop below, and then hold on.

Few big fish hang or feed with smaller fish.

These anglers are usually using a weighted treble hook that can cause problems when trying to hook a big fish. Also, many times the bigger fish are sitting just behind the school feeding and not necessarily right

Swarming gulls are a sure indication of fish feeding on the surface. Here, the stripers have driven a school of small sea herring to the surface in early spring and the gulls have joined in on the action.

On calm days, you can easily spot menhaden schools by the telltale ripples they make on the surface as they move. The more tightly packed the school of menhaden is, the higher the probability there are predators beneath it.

COLOR CHANGES AND SCUM LINES

Many gamefish gather where muddy water meets cleaner, clearer water. This can be from a river flowing down and entering a channel or from runoff where a flat meets some deeper water after a storm. Fish will hold on the edge of a color change and ambush bait that comes out of the muddy or roiled water. Prime areas are where this color change goes over or meets some distinct feature along the bottom, such as rocks or gravel. Color changes can also occur on a beach, where the light-colored shallow water darkens as it becomes deeper.

Scum lines that have grass, weeds, debris, plastic bottles, small pieces of wood, and other items floating along their length will form from water being pushed up and onto the shoreline by big tides, which then drag back all that junk when they begin to recede. The scum will follow the normal current back into the deeper water. This will usually attract and hold smaller bait, such as shrimp, silversides, and crabs, and stripers will hold on either side of the line, picking off the bait. Scum lines will also help you pinpoint the direction and speed of the current and what it is moving by or over. A scum line can lead you to many more productive fishing areas if you follow what it's telling you.

beneath the school. I find that reeling in the bait and re-hooking it to a different rod, set up with a weight above the hook to take it to the bottom, is a lot better. I like to re-hook the bait on a big #5/0 to #7/0 single hook or a #2/0 to #4/0 treble hook, a length of leader about 24 inches long with a barrel swivel at the top, and an egg sinker of appropriate weight above that. That way the fish feels less weight when he takes the bait, and nothing interferes with the hook gap.

CHAPTER 2

FLATS

WHEN I WAS A YOUNG BOY and would fish with my father and grandfather, we would sometimes arrive at an area in our boat and see gulls and terns wheeling, screeching, and diving over the water close to shore. *Why were those birds diving over the water so close to shore, and were they above fish?* I would ask. Their answer was always the same: *No!* Even at that young age, I had already been taught to look for feeding birds, as that would likely indicate fish feeding beneath them. That was, of course, as long as the water wasn't too shallow and the birds weren't too close to shore. They would say that the water was too shallow and that the birds were feeding on dead crabs, small fish, or other floating debris.

Most flats are best fished on rising water and during low-light conditions, such as dawn or dusk.

At that time, the basic rule was that if you wanted to catch striped bass on the flats, even smaller schoolies, you had to fish just before sunrise, just before sunset, or during the night. At any other time, you needed a boat and you only fished in deep water. Always. You had to

TV host Cindy Garrison casts to some big shallow-water stripers aboard *White Ghost 2* in a shallow back bay.

steer clear of those shallow-water areas, as they not only were barren of fish but also dangerous to boats and boaters.

In their defense, during those days the boats available to most fishermen were made of wood, were heavy, and usually drew a lot more water than today's fiberglass or aluminum boats. There also wasn't the option of quickly raising your engine with a power-trim unit to get the lower unit out of harm's way. (Even if that option had been available, it would certainly have been a luxury that most blue-collar workers could not afford.) So there were some practical reasons to avoid shallow water. Also, at that time, the ocean was so full of fish there was no need to venture beyond the places you were used to finding and catching them.

Today, we now know that striped bass do indeed move into low-water areas and that some areas can hold huge fish at various times of the year and during different tidal stages. What's become known as flats fishing throughout the striper's range is still in its infancy, and I do not think we totally understand exactly what takes place in these shoreline

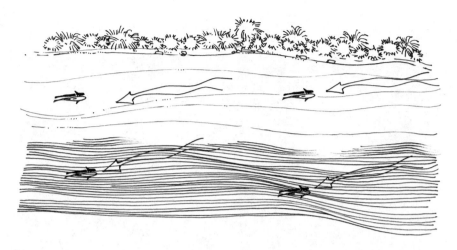

If there is a good rip or a strong current, cast up-tide and let your lure, bait, or fly come down with the current naturally. The fish will be facing into the tide and looking for food coming from that direction.

areas. So I never assume that the water is too shallow or that I am too far back in a cove, river, creek, or estuary. When I ran a Florida-style flats boat in my guide business, I'd see stripers slip just inches beneath the boat, swimming out and off to safer depths as the tide dropped. If there's a lot of bait in the area, bass will go as shallow as necessary to feed, sometimes into water so low their backs and fins stick out of the water. They'll feed until the water becomes too low to swim in, and then they'll fall back into safer haunts.

> The shallower you fish, the faster your retrieve should be; when fishing in deeper water, slow down your retrieve.

The biggest striped bass that we have ever taken while fishing a flat has been 46 pounds, 7 ounces, and it was caught after dark on a live eel. The biggest fish taken during the day with the sun out was 38 pounds, 11 ounces, and that fish ate a 7-inch Red Fin swimmer reeled slowly across the surface in the spring. If you aren't fishing the flats on a regular basis, especially in the spring of the year, then you are without a doubt missing one of the better big-fish areas that get little or no pressure in many areas.

USING CHARTS

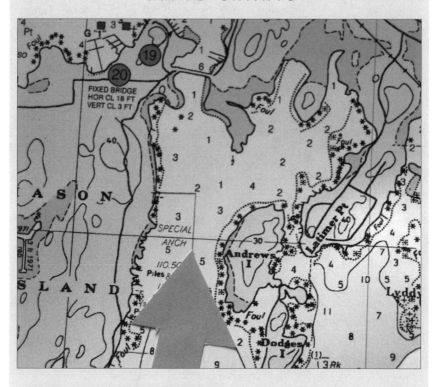

A good nautical chart is the best way to find flats. Flats will usually appear on charts as large sections of fairly even water depths. Look for low-water readings to see where 1- to 3-foot markings appear over a fairly large area. On some charts, the shallower water will be colored green or a light shade of blue to distinguish it from the nearby deeper water.

Flats do not have to be vast expanses of sand, mud, or gravel. I know of at least three flats that, when placed together, wouldn't equal a hundred acres, and there are always fish feeding, cruising, and sunning on each one. There usually aren't any other fishermen or boaters there either. When looking at one of these flats from shore or from a boat, your first impression would be that the area couldn't possibly hold any fish. But you'd be wrong. There are countless small flats just waiting to be discovered. All you need to do is look for them.

Features of Flats

Flats that have some sort of weed cover, rock, mussels, or green cabbage grass on the bottom usually hold fish much longer in the spring because that dark bottom debris heats up quicker than the surrounding areas and also make the flat more hospitable to microorganisms, worms, crabs, shrimp, silversides, and more. Stripers will grub through this bottom cover looking for food.

When such areas are adjacent to white sand, fish find cover in these darker areas when they arrive on a flat. Consider what you would do if you were trying to hide from someone. Would you sit out in the middle of an area of pure white sand, or would you hide behind a rock or some grass or in a hole so you could jump out and surprise your target?

Captain Ryan Sansoucy of Hush Fly Fishing Charters is prepared for a day of sight-fishing for stripers. The face mask, sunglasses, and brimmed hat not only provide critical sun protection but also reduce glare and enhance his ability to spot fish.

Even a slight drop-off provides safety and a great ambush area for a striper. Bigger stripers will wait at the edge of a flat, where the shallow water falls off to deeper water (in some areas this drop-off can be as little as a couple of feet, whereas in others it can be 20 feet or more) to intercept baitfish as they are forced over the top of the flat and into deeper water.

When stripers first arrive on flats of soft, cream-colored sand, they stand out against the light bottom and are easy to sight-cast to. However, once they have been on the flat for awhile, they will tend to take on the lighter coloration of the bottom and are harder to see as they move across the sand.

Other flats may be made up of mud, small stones, clay, shells, or mussel or oyster beds. All are worth exploring. In general, sand flats will hold more types of baitfish. Flats made up of soft mud will usually provide for good worm swarms when conditions are right. Gravel, stone, and shell flats harbor crabs, small lobster, mussels, shrimp, and other types of crustaceans.

Once you are on a flat, look for subtle bottom changes as you move along. Try to find anything that appears different from the surrounding area: small weed patches, grass, a single rock, some gravel, or small contours. Like when fishing other bodies of water, only 10 percent of the water will hold 90 percent of the fish. The best times to find the areas that hold bait and gamefish are not when you are fishing. Go out and look around at different times of the year and at different stages of the tide for the sole purpose of reconnaissance.

Flats are not only prime feeding spots, but stripers also use them

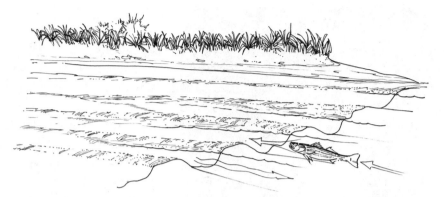

Stripers use flats as traveling lanes. On almost any flat, there are slight differences in the bottom contours along its length. The change might be only a few inches in depth but can sometimes be two feet or more. Fish will follow these slight depressions the same way we follow highways.

as traveling lanes to and from feeding areas. Depressions as little as 6 inches can be superhighways, and fish will follow them religiously as the tide rises and falls. On almost any flat, there are slight differences in the bottom contours along its length. The change might be only a few inches in depth, but can sometimes be a couple of feet or more.

When to Fish the Flats

In the early season, stripers head for the flats to feed on silversides, glass minnows, bay anchovies, shrimp, crabs, and other bait that will at some point usually feed and breed on the flat. In the fall, stripers again hunt the flats. Most of the baitfish are now fully grown, they are usually plentiful, and the stripers come looking for them before they begin to migrate. In our area, in the spring you may get eight to ten weeks of good fishing; in the fall you'll be lucky to get half that. September and October line storms, low-pressure systems that arrive one after another, bringing strong wind, lots of rain, and a drop in barometric pressure can kill the fishing if the sea never gets a chance to calm down, clean up, and get back to normal. However, some good action can occur for a small window before these storms arrive or after they pass.

Capt. Jim White holds a big striper that ate a live eel in four feet of water while fishing with Capt. Joe Pagano. Capt. Pagano has built an entire business of fishing live eels in shallow water for striped bass and does it both day and night with tremendous success.

The accepted theory is that flats are best fished on a rising tide and that the fish depart as the water begins to recede, but some flats don't fish well until the water has fallen for one, two, or even three hours. On other flats, only an incoming tide will bring fish, and usually once high water arrives, they quickly depart. Some great-looking flats don't attract any fish. Other flats only fish well for small fish. You have to learn each flat's little quirks and secrets.

For many, sight-fishing the flats when the sun is high is flats fishing at its finest. You see the fish and can watch the silver flash when a big fish turns sideways to feed and its mouth opens wide to swallow your lure. The whole key to spotting fish is to wear quality sunglasses and a hat with a dark brim to reduce glare. High quality glasses allow you to spot cruising fish, as well as offer good UV protection. Those with side-shields block light coming in from the sides. Fish with the sun to your back or over your shoulder if you are going to sight-cast to fish. This reduces glare, which increases your ability to spot fish. Don't look straight down into the water; you will miss too much of what is actually going on. Instead, train yourself to look out and down at an angle into the water. Once you master this technique, you will be amazed at how many fish you will see. Sometimes the fish will appear as a dark blotch or patch against the bottom. Stripers, especially the bigger ones, can blend into the bottom with amazing ease.

While I have had great fishing on sunny days, I have had even better fishing in low light—early morning, late evening, cloudy days, rainy days, and foggy days. On nights when there isn't a lot of wind, flats can come alive with baitfish and big predators. Anglers that shun night fishing because it's challenging are missing some of the best fishing of

Justin White holds a beautiful bass taken on a flat at night. Make sure you know the area well before venturing out in the dark. Check it out during the day to make sure you know where any rocks or obstructions are so you can fish it safely at night.

the year, especially in the spring, when the fish feed heavily on a fairly regular basis. At night you have a distinct advantage over large stripers. One flat that I usually take fly-fishing clients to during the day produces good numbers of smaller stripers. However, I will return after dark with a party and toss live eels in the same area and consistently catch fish in the 30-pound range. Those who have gone with me at both times have been totally amazed by how the area changes after the sun goes down.

Darkness offers a completely different range of sensory sensations. Hearing the fish slurp, pop, and swish while they feed is exciting, especially when all is still and quiet. Then suddenly a fish strikes your lure or bait, rips line from your reel, and sends a heart-stopping electric shock down the line. A 25-pound fish hooked on the flats is a completely different animal than the same size fish hooked in deeper water.

Locating Fish

While fishing flats, pay close attention to any signs of feeding fish or other fish activity. Cast to small baitfish that suddenly jump clear of the water, which may signal a predator beneath. Also look for fins exposed on the surface or tailing fish that are grubbing in the sand and mud for crabs or other bait. You may only see such indications for a second or two before they disappear.

Once you do see a fin or a noticeable wake, usually in the form of distinct V, remember that the fish is most likely at least a foot or two ahead of what you are looking at. You want to place your lure or fly two or three feet ahead of the fish so that it intercepts it. Since most flats are totally featureless, it's important—once you spot or catch a few fish—to quickly mark your location using your GPS or drop a marker. That way, you can return to the marker after you have drifted away.

Releasing stripers in shallow water takes a bit of time and patience. Make sure the fish is ready before you let it go.

Capt. Rick Ruoff holds a nice striper he caught on a fly. Capt. Ruoff filmed one of his ESPN shows with us and was impressed with the numbers of big fish we found on flats during our shoot together.

Gulls, terns, and cormorants—and even shoreline egrets—will give away the bait's position in the water. If you arrive at a flat and there are dozens of birds just spread out and sitting on the water, that usually indicates that some type of feeding has just taken place and very well could happen again. Stick around for awhile and watch—the fish may just come back up and start feeding again.

Bigger stripers will wait at the edge of a flat, where the shallow water falls off to deeper water (in some areas this drop-off can be as little as two feet; in others it can be 20 feet or more) to intercept baitfish as they are forced over the top of the flat and into deeper water. The steeper the drop, the more large fish. If the water is very deep, fish the area with jigs or deep-swimming plugs. Bump the jig or lure off of the top of the flat so it causes the sand or mud to puff. As your lure comes into the deeper water, a striper will usually be there waiting for it. Flats close to deep water will usually be cooler than ones farther away from deep water. The tide brings cooler water onto the flats from the nearby deeper water, providing much better fishing for a longer period of time.

A flat with a stream or creek dumping into it can be a tremendous hot spot when the tide begins to fall and bait are pulled out of the creek and onto the flat. Water that supports river herring in the spring can be some of the best areas of all. Those big herring will be going back

Nick Curcione releases a fly-rod striper after spotting some jumping baitfish in shallow water. Being observant can increase your catch.

and forth trying to ascend the river to spawn, as well as using it as they leave to return to the sea. Use bigger swimmers like seven-inch Red Fins, Tattoo Swimmers, and other types of surface swimming lures that leave a good-size wake as you reel them back in.

Do not waste a lot of time repeatedly casting to the same area. In most cases, the fish are either there or not. Experience has taught me that if I haven't located fish after ten minutes or so, they are in another area of the flat. Lures such as poppers, Zara Spooks, Rat-L-Traps, and plastic shad bodies on jigheads are good for covering water to find fish quickly. I like to use a longer rod (8- to 9-foot spinning rod and 12- or 15-pound-test monofilament) that casts farther than shorter rods to cover the flat from farther away, which is especially beneficial if you are fishing from a standard center-console boat that doesn't have a shallow draft. With long casts, I cover a lot of water and can quickly establish whether there are feeding fish on the flat. Once I find them, I'll often switch to a fly or other method for a more precise approach. The time saved can translate into more fish in the boat.

Dealing with Wind

Wind can push your boat too fast, making it difficult to get a good retrieve. Rather than use a trolling motor to control the speed of the boat, I prefer to anchor, use a drag chain, or deploy a sea anchor or wind sock to slow down the drift. Lefty Kreh taught me how to use a drag chain, which is nothing more than a length of ¾-inch chain with a long line attached to it. You let out enough line so the chain drags on the bottom and slows you down. When the drag chain is tied off the bow, the boat will drift in a straight line as the wind pushes it along. As the chain drags the bottom, it kicks up mud and dust, dislodging worms, shrimp, and other food, which also attracts fish to the boat.

A drift sock is a cone-shaped piece of vinyl or canvas that is attached to the stern with a rope and dragged in the water behind the boat. Water collects in the sock, slowing down your boat. I'd go up one or two sizes larger than what the manufacturer recommends for your boat.

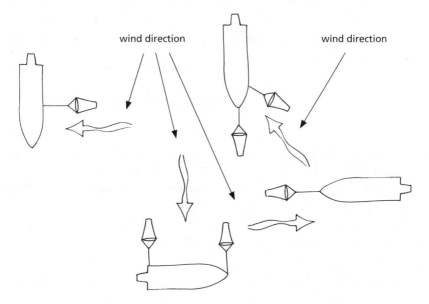

You can use two or more sea anchors to get precise boat control if it is windy. This allows you to keep your main motor turned off and drift quietly, which is important in shallow water.

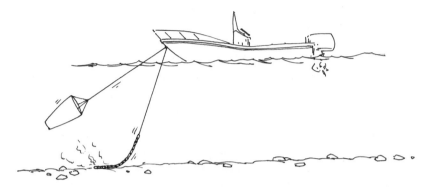

Make a simple drag chain from 6- to 8-foot long, ¾-inch chain attached to a rope. Release enough line to slow the drift of your boat. If you point your bow into the wind and put the chain down off the bow, your boat will drift slow and straight as the wind pushes you along.

Whenever I've purchased the recommended size, it hasn't helped slow down my boat at all. Depending on the size of your boat, two bags— one off of the bow and one off of the stern—may be better than one. Now you can drift pretty much in the exact direction that you want to go. Freshwater anglers who fish the Great Lakes for all different types of species have used this method successfully for years. Somehow it has never really become popular in salt water.

Sound and Stealth

When fishing from a boat, many anglers don't notice the tackle, bait containers, pails, rods, and soda cans that fall onto the deck. Shore anglers thrash and splash through the water, kicking up as much water as a Jet Ski. Silently, the fish have been hearing and feeling everything you and your buddies have been doing.

Based on my personal observations, I think that stripers can hear sounds that are transmitted through the water, such as the slap of a waves against the hull of a boat or a motor going in and out of gear or a splash on the surface, as well as sounds that originate in the air and are transmitted through the water, such as loud voices.

A striper can detect sound from a combination of its inner ear, through its lateral line—capable of picking up low-frequency sound

Bass can easily pick up strange sounds, noises, and vibrations, so it's important to be quiet when fishing. Sound reverberates off of the bottom as well as off the rocks below and will alert any big fish in the area that something is not right. *Mike Laptew photo*

from a great distances—and by amplifying sounds with their swim-bladders. Through these senses, sound waves (which travel approximately 4.5 times faster than through air) are transferred to the pea-size brain of the fish to process. The larger the fish, the greater its survival instincts have been honed and the more refined and sharpened its feeding habits have become. Whether you fish from a boat or wade the shoreline, if you are looking to catch a big striper, you had better learn pretty quickly to be quiet.

When possible, anchor your boat and wade. You'll create less noise that way.

When I owned a Florida-style flats boat, I would stand atop the poling platform all day long and observe how the fish would react to my clients' talking and any sudden movements aboard the boat or engine noise. I used to maneuver very slowly, using the main engine to get in

A bass chasing a baitfish in shallow water hones in on its prey quickly. Underwater cameraman Mike Laptew snapped this photo of a nice bass getting ready to eat this baitfish. *Mike Laptew photo*

tight to shallow-water flats or shorelines, but not any longer. I will now use a trolling motor or a push-pole to move the boat around in shallow water and a wind sock or drag chain to control its drift. If I want to fish a particular spot, I'll anchor and let out enough rope to place me where I want to be, or even beach the boat and wade, depending on the prevailing conditions. Continually starting up your engine to reposition yourself makes a lot of unnecessary noise. Wade into the current and the wind so any mud or sand you kick up will be carried away behind you and not toward the fish ahead, alerting them to your presence.

Even using a trolling motor can spook stripers. The fish respond to the low electric pulse and hum of the engine by moving quickly out of the area. If they are feeding heavily, as in the spring and fall, they may not pay as close attention to this sound, but if they have just arrived in shallow water or if it's mid to late summer and they have been chased and harassed for weeks on end, they'll head for the deeper water in a hurry.

When conditions prevented using an electric motor or push-pole, I'd anchor my flats boat up-current or upwind from where I wanted to

This bass fell for a vibrating shad-tail bait in 5 feet of water. Swim shads like this one vibrate in the water and attract fish. They are one of the easiest lures to learn how to use since the action is already built into the bait.

be and then feed out additional anchor line a bit at a time to cover the area more thoroughly, as clam diggers do when they are covering an area. The technique allows you to let your boat drift back 100 to 200 feet very slowly and silently and will usually get you more fish than hauling anchor and motoring to a new spot.

When fishing a flat from a boat, any movement inside the boat should be kept to a minimum, especially during the day, when the fish can see you as well. Fish that are moving toward you will quickly turn away if they see you. Try to keep as low a profile as possible when fishing during the day, especially when the sun is high in the sky.

Waves slapping against your boat hull—especially on an aluminum boat—put you at a distinct disadvantage when fishing a flat since the waves reverberate beneath the water's surface. The fish will hear this. More than once I've seen anglers in aluminum skiffs catching fish after fish, only to get shut down when the wind came up. They all

Stealth in shallow water leads to nice fish. So move quietly and carefully—especially in back coves or creeks.

believed that the fish had left the area or simply stopped feeding. If I waited ten minutes or so and returned to the same location, the fish were once again feeding. The fish hadn't moved at all; they were simply alerted by the strange sound and became wary. In very shallow water a safe escape is usually some distance away, so they are already on guard for anything that seems unusual. You can improve your aluminum boat by placing carpet on the deck to muffle the sound inside. I've seen some boats where the owner has even glued carpeting to the side of his boat, covering the chines, so when the water hits it, it doesn't make any loud splashing sounds against the aluminum.

Shifting your outboard motor in and out of gear can be heard as far as 60 feet below the water's surface.

I had the benefit of getting a little bit of insight into sound and the underwater world through underwater videography. My friend Mike Laptew has produced dozens of videos on fish behavior and has stud-

By placing rattles inside plastic lures and flies you can up the odds of catching more fish. Freshwater anglers have been doing this for years.

ied them extensively. His work has appeared on television and he has worked for *National Geographic*. Mike is free diver who can hold his breath for up to three minutes or more and regularly dives to 50, 60, or 70 feet, without an oxygen tank. This gives him the opportunity to get close to fish without spooking them.

On one particular dive, his goal was to capture images of a big bass hitting an eel near the bottom next to a huge rock. The water was roughly 60-feet deep. Mike went down and began to film from the bottom up toward the surface. The angler in the boat above lowered his eel and began what's called "stemming the tide," putting his outboard motor in and out of gear to keep himself directly over the rock below. When we watched Mike's footage, not only could you hear the hum of the big outboard above, but also a distinctive click, click, click as the engine went from forward to reverse. And the video camera was inside a waterproof protective housing 60 feet beneath the surface.

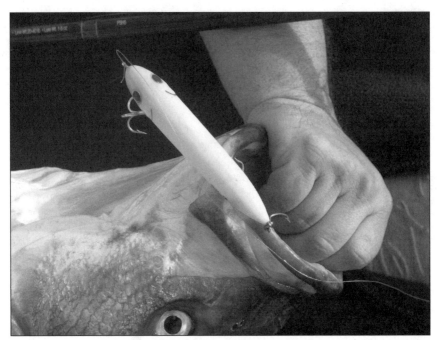

On a dropping tide, a cream-colored Zara Spook fooled this striper that was holding close to the drop-off. Zara Spooks have the ability to bring fish out of deep water to the surface on almost any occasion. It's an excellent choice for calm water, and the built-in rattles get more attention from fish in dirty water, as well.

I have also watched stripers react to the sound of voices, whether it was my own giving instructions to a client or an excited client talking loudly. Many times this sound stops the fish dead in their tracks. I know some people say that fish can't hear human voices, but I have serious doubts about this.

On one occasion while fishing with Capt. Joe Pagano, we were returning from fishing the coastline at mid-morning when we ran into a massive school of menhaden in the channel at the entrance of the harbor. We decided to get some baitfish shots, so we lowered our waterproof video camera down about 3 feet or so below the surface and began filming.

As we drifted with the current, I kept the camera as far beneath the surface as I possibly could. All of a sudden, a second boat approached.

A nice bass comes alongside after eating a big Lefty's Deceiver that it swallowed in one gulp. Large flies will usually attract large fish, but not always.

It was 75 to 100 feet off our stern when the boat's captain yelled over to us, "Hey! What kind of fish are these that I see beneath my boat?" Joe answered, "Baby menhaden." As they conversed back and forth, I continued to film the massive school of bait beneath us. When we got home that evening and replayed the tape to see how much useable footage we'd shot, we were amazed to hear that the camera's microphone had picked up the other captain's voice as clear as a bell. Each and every word was audible, and the boat was almost 100 feet away from us and our camera was submerged three feet.

Now, I know that there is a difference between what the microphone picks up and what the fish can hear, but I firmly believe that they can detect the sound from voices. Topics such as this aren't really written about too much as they are complicated and solely based on scientific data. But when I see fish disperse or run, after a couple of guys are yelling their heads off, my eyes and brain tells me there has to be some sort of connection and that they sensed something.

One fishing situation that I see over and over is when an angler is reeling in a hooked fish close to the boat, and that hooked fish is being followed by two or three other fish. Their curiosity got the best of them, and perhaps they are investigating why their brother is struggling, hoping to cash in on what he's feeding on. Many times, we get another fly or lure to them and catch those fish that are following the unlucky one in. But often the partner of the lucky angler will yell, "Hey look at those fish," and the following fish will quickly turn and run. Was it because they saw the boat? Perhaps. But one thing is true, when I tell my clients to be quiet, those trailing fish don't scatter as fast.

Adding rattles to your flies, lures, or soft plastics, will help fish home in on them, especially in cloudy or muddy water.

Based on these unscientific observations, I think that there is a high probability that fish can detect our voices. You can yell and scream to your heart's content. As for me, I'll remain as quiet as possible. At the end of the day, we can see who catches the most fish.

CHAPTER 3

POINTS:
BIG-FISH MAGNETS

I HAVE LONG BELIEVED that saltwater fishermen could learn a lot from their freshwater counterparts. Many saltwater anglers have a run-and-gun approach to fishing in the brine. I myself have been guilty of this tactic and have to constantly remind myself to slow down and think about what I'm doing. This was made very clear when I fished with Shaw Grigsby while filming his TV show, *One More Cast*.

The first areas that we fished were points in Narragansett Bay, but though I regularly fished these areas, that was where the similarities ended. His approach was methodical and scientific. As we approached a point, he had already decided on what direction we'd begin, where we'd start and how far away, the lures for the job, and considered the prevailing conditions. All this from a guy who had never set eyes on Narragansett Bay. We fished the areas that were obvious to me, but we also fished some that weren't. In the end we caught fish where I had never fished before, and I'd been fishing these waters since I was old enough to walk. It was a shocking revelation to have someone who'd

This rocky outcropping shows the high-water mark along the rocks. When the tide recedes, a rip is formed as it rounds the tip of the rocks, and stripers will ambush bait on the inside corners.

never laid eyes on this body of water, let alone a freshwater angler, to take me to school in just three short days. One of the qualities that impressed me most about Shaw was his ability to look at the shoreline, then refer to our Lowrance GPS mapping system, and immediately determine not only if we should bother fishing that point but also how to fish it, what approach to make, and what the bottom composition would be like based on land and map features.

Approach each spot as if it were filled with big bass.

Points in shallow water are one of the easiest types of structure to find, both on a chart and visually, and can hold some very big fish. Points jut out into the water in back bays, river systems, estuaries, around islands and especially off of the mainland itself. Many of these points are fishable; however, not all points will be as productive at all times across the entire season, and some will almost never hold any fish. Your job is to locate and determine the best points for monster stripers.

Proximity to Deep Water

The best points have a sharp change in water depth close by that provides big fish with a place to hide and rest in between feeding periods. Points near channels or rips are great areas to find big stripers lying in wait. Here, baitfish will become trapped, disoriented, and tossed about by the increasing tide and current as it begins to drop. Some points are nothing more than sandbars jutting out from the shoreline. Bars that do not fall off into deeper water and just taper off slowly are not as productive as ones with steep drop-offs, unless they have other good features.

Points with some sort of structure, such as eelgrass or shoreline grass, mussel beds, oyster beds, rocks or rock piles, old pilings, and other types of natural or man-made structures, are big-fish hangouts,

Learning how to use different types of gear and equipment will make you a better angler. Bass pro Shaw Grigsby shows he's no stranger to fly fishing. He landed this 16-pound bass off a shallow-water point.

A point that juts out and away from land will usually hold bass somewhere along it. Notice the calm water and wind rip line. The fish will be close to the disturbed water on the surface looking for bait passing by. Approach points slowly and quietly, fishing both sides and the tip. Study charts to find out if there is any hidden structure nearby that bass may use.

especially in the early morning and late evening. When the tide is moving at those times of the day, the structure provides the fish with feeding zones and lanes to move between deep water and shallow.

Use and study a good NOAA chart of the area you plan on fishing. This chart will give you a wealth of information on bottom composition, drop-offs, channels, structure, and any nearby wrecks. The slope and the shape of the point you can see extends much farther out under the water's surface. With a good chart, you can figure out just how far out the point extends and how steep the slope actually is. In back bays and harbors, the gradual slope of a point usually extends far into the water. However, strong currents and or rips can eat the bottom away from the water constantly flowing back and forth, creating a sharp drop-off. The closer the lines are on the chart, the steeper the drop.

Always fish the windward side of a point.

Fish the Windy Side of Points

For as long as I can remember, anglers have been advised to fish the windy side of a point, but few pay much attention to this advice. Most of us fear the wind and don't want to deal with it, opting instead to fish the calm, windless side, as it presents fewer headaches. Yes, it's true that being blown into shore in a boat is a hassle, and casting into the wind while standing in the surf isn't easy. But windy points are better than calm points for a number of reasons. First, the wind and wave action cuts the light penetration from above, which gives bigger fish a sense of security and allows them to move in close and higher up toward the point than they might normally. Second, the wind forces plankton toward the shoreline, which in turn, draws baitfish that feed on it. Stripers will usually follow the baitfish into the shallows. The wind can also cause a back-eddy on a point on the opposite side from which it is blowing. For example, if the wind is blowing from left to

Billy Nolan lands a nice bass he caught from a point with a wind rip line. Wind rips can develop in an instant and last for only a short period of time, so you need to pay attention.

Angler Gip Sission, who has won many tournaments, holds a 50-pound striper he caught on a new moon tide in early summer. Gip has accounted for many big fish by learning to fish the proper tides at the right time.

right, an eddy will form on the right side of the point when the wind is against the tide and current. Regardless of the eddy's size, all stripers will seek out this turbulence.

One area inside our bay has three points in a row, spaced about 150 yards apart. Between them are many small reefs and rock piles surrounded by sand, making for an excellent transition zone. On any given day you can catch a couple of fish here, a couple there, and then move on. However, when the wind blows hard from the southeast and is pushing water toward the shoreline and creating good wave action, the area lights up like a Christmas tree. The fish will be right against the shoreline feeding like mad. They are so close you actually have to cast your plug up on the shore and pull it off into the water to get a strike. While it is hard to fish and control the boat in such conditions, the rewards are worth the effort. In eighteen years of guiding in that area, I have never seen *any* boats fishing there when the wind is hard out of the southeast. Most leave and go find somewhere easier to fish.

Stripers will hold on the outside points of rock jetties as well as in eddies that form along the insides of the structures.

Go in slowly and quietly when approaching a point and fish the adjacent water from the top to the bottom to find where the fish are holding and feeding.

When approaching a point, fish the deep water first and then the shallow water as you move in closer. The fish could be anywhere in between. Do not overlook the eddies on the inside corners of points.

Bass often herd and trap bait on the inside corners of points, making it easier for them to feed. Corners closest to deep water or near some current or a channel are better than the shallower ones. Also, look for nearby cover, such as grass or rocks.

Many anglers motor up too close and too fast to a point, using their main engine and scaring any big fish that are feeding in close. Cut that engine and use a trolling motor to get in tight, or drift in with the wind and the tide. Secondly, anglers do not pay close attention to the wind, the tide, or any signs of baitfish in the area before they go plowing in to fish. Begin casting on the outside areas, which are deeper, and work your way in close slowly. This is when it pays to know where the deep water is before you get there. It's also the very reason that you should be studying your charts to locate those areas before you arrive. As you approach from the deeper water, dredge those depths as you move in closer to the point, and keep noise to a minimum.

Points in Rivers

On a dropping tide, fish will converge on the opposite side of the point, out of the main flow of the current, and wait for the bait to be swept over the top of the point. Points deflect and concentrate the water, increasing its speed. Pay close attention to any slack water—stripers will ambush unsuspecting baitfish here after they become disoriented in the stronger tidal flow.

Most coves and rivers will have trees or high banks that provide shade as the sun rises higher in the sky. Big stripers just love to lie in the shade of such areas, especially early and late in the day, which is the best time to fish points. On cloudy or overcast days, the bite may last a lot longer, especially on days when there is a light and steady rain with little or no wind. Such weather might be a bit uncomfortable, but it is one of the best times to be out fishing. Cover the water column from the surface to the bottom thoroughly. Also, fish tend to

Shorelines facing east with high tree lines on them and rock structure below offer shade for a longer period of time during the day. This will keep the bass closer to the shore for an extended time, allowing you to fish longer.

Hall of Fame angler and *Outdoor Life* fishing editor Jerry Gibbs holding a nice bass he took on a fly rod. Fishing with a legendary angler like Jerry is like going to school again.

drop back to deeper water as the sun rises higher in the sky. Once you have learned their habits and travel lanes, you can ambush them.

Points near streams that empty into the main body of water are good place to fish also. A point that reaches deep water, like a channel, is one of the very best points to target. Gamefish will move from the deeper water area to the shallower water to feed early and late in the day. When another "break-line" comes in between the shallower water and the deeper water, the bigger stripers will hold on that feature to feed and will usually not move any higher up onto the point. This feature could be as shallow as three or four feet, so probe the area with jigs or deeper-running lures. Remember that the current at the bottom is not as strong as it is at the top. Use your trolling motor to get in close. If you don't have one, or one that is not powerful enough, use a sea anchor (drift sock) or drag chain to slow down your drift (see page 37).

Fly Fishing Points

Approach the point with two rods ready to go—one with a sinking line and one with floating or intermediate line—so that you can cover the same water from deep to shallow as effectively as someone using spinning or casting gear. The deeper water adjacent to most points is usually no more than 15 feet or so, so it's well within the range of most fly tackle.

Choose your flies carefully before you begin fishing the area. Start on the outside with a

Approach points slowly and begin fishing from the outside in.

weighted Clouser Deep Minnow, and be ready to toss a big Deceiver or some other baitfish pattern as you move in closer. Having your rods rigged and ready to go will save a lot of precious time as you begin to fish the area, and you won't have to worry about tying on flies or changing leaders before you begin to fish.

CHAPTER 4

TIDAL RIVERS

THE MANY TIDAL RIVERS along our coastline offer shallow-water anglers the opportunity to catch big stripers. They also offer the average guy with a small boat or no boat at all a vast area of territory to fish and explore. Once you decipher some of a river's many secrets, she'll reward you with nice fish.

Tidal rivers and tidal creeks are some of the most productive and dynamic systems along the entire striper coastline. This is where most saltwater life-forms are born and grow before moving out into the ocean. The shores and bottom of a tidal river are usually alive with all types of plants, fish, crustaceans, and other types of life. The food chain begins in tidal rivers, and almost all species of saltwater fish will at some time spawn or feed in them.

Rivers are loaded with feeding stations. Especially in the spring and fall, rivers are usually full with food. In the spring, bass chase alewives or American eel that are migrating upriver, and in the fall, they maraud the young as they make their way back to sea. During the summer, stripers will usually go upriver at night to feed and drop back to deeper water before the sun rises.

Lefty Kreh holds a 37-pound striper taken on the Susquehanna Flats in the spring on a big Deceiver. Up and down the coast, big fish will move into shallow-water areas in the spring. *Lefty Kreh photo*

When the tide drops, baitfish are forced out of the creek and onto the flat. When this happens, large stripers take notice.

Fish feed far upriver as the incoming tide washes over flats. When fishing a tidal river, fish as far upstream as you can, dropping back as the tide recedes. The goal is to follow the fish as they move with the tide. Prime spots for fish are flats in front of feeder creeks, points, deep cut banks, and other structure.

Not all river fish will be huge. This schoolie decided to try and swallow a 10-inch Fin-S Fish. In most cases you can't use a lure or a fly that is too big for a striper to try and eat it. This little guy drives that point home. Try to imagine what it was thinking when it tried to eat this big bait.

Rivers can have small and large coves, bridges, channels, creeks, sand and mud flats, rock formations, points, pilings, grass beds, and more. All this fish-holding structure and diverse topography packed tightly into one small area can be hard to figure out, no matter your experience level. There are so many places for stripers to hide, feed, and rest that deciding on where to begin looking can be a difficult and time-consuming process. The anglers that get good at fishing rivers spend lifetimes learning their secrets.

Always fish the mouths of feeder creeks, streams, and smaller rivers.

Like the search for big fish everywhere, you'll have to forgo the fun of catching lots of fish. That's one part of this game that a lot of anglers have a problem with. They run into a pile of small fish that are aggressive and hitting everything thrown at them, and they then put finding and catching a big fish on the back burner.

Fishing the Tides

Almost all rivers fish best when the tide begins to recede. Prime time happens when a high tide occurs an hour or two before sunrise. There is something about an early-morning dropping tide that stripers seem to love. Since this only occurs a few times each month, it's up to you to be there at the right time.

Big stripers will move up into a river to look for baitfish that have gathered during the night. When a high tide occurs in the wee hours of the morning, while it's still dark, stripers ascend the river on the rising water, using the cover of darkness as protection, and disperse over a wide area as the tide covers the flats and allows the baitfish to enter their grassy defenses to hide from hungry predators.

Normally in high-water conditions during the day or early evening, you should fish as far upriver as you can get. Once the tide begins to ebb and drop, you then follow it back down to the river mouth. If

This big bass ate a Bass Kandy Delight in a tidal river on a dropping tide. These long, thin shads are deadly on big bass, as are Hogy's lures, Slug-Gos, and a host of other big plastic baits.

Mike Laptew tries to stop a big striper from reaching the rocks while fishing a big 12-inch Slug-Go. This new giant Slug-Go attracts big fish almost anywhere and at anytime.

you find a concentration of fish far upriver and then the bite suddenly tapers off or ends, begin to move downriver and start checking areas of structure. Chances are you will find the fish as they move down with the dropping tide. If you wait too long to make this move, you could totally miss the bite farther downriver. The speed of the tide and the current will dictate how fast and how far the stripers move downriver.

At low tide, especially the last two hours or so of a dropping tide, the stripers that remain will stack up in a small area. The challenge is finding them. Deep-cut banks, channel drop-offs, and troughs will all hold stripers at low water, as well as pilings, piers, rock piles, islands, and mud flats that lie next to deep water. It usually requires a lot of time, effort, and patience to get these fish to hit. If you can find a river or creek that has an alewife run, then fish this area hard on falling tides later in the spring when the alewives are heading back to sea.

Structure

Have a set plan on which types of structure you are going to fish. Points, sandbars, rock piles, bridges, and flats will likely hold feeding fish as well as those waiting to intercept baitfish swept downstream as the current pulls them away from nearshore sanctuaries.

Not all areas hold big stripers all of the time. In most areas, you are likely to find more school-size stripers and very few monsters. This is the part of the puzzle you need to figure out. The bigger fish can be in many different places at many different times, depending on the river system. Looking for all these fish-holding areas is only the first part of actually figuring out where the stripers are going to be. In one river system, such as the Susquehanna River in the Chesapeake Bay, you may regularly catch big stripers on the flats in the spring. In the Northeast that might not happen at all, or if it does, the bite may not last long. Each river system has its own quirks and special set of

The Slug-Go is the original "Stick Bait" developed by Herb Reed of Lunker City Lures and was voted one of the top-ten best lures of all time by *Outdoor Life*. 9- and 12-inch Slug-Gos are good for working tidal rivers for big stripers, and I wouldn't go fishing without them.

This bass ate an old Google Eye swimmer fished next to a bridge abutment in the dark shadow line. Surface swimmers, both old and new, work great when fishing next to bridges. Let them swim with the current toward the abutments for a natural presentation.

problems. All we can do is to begin studying rivers in general terms and go from there. So what works in Rhode Island might not necessarily work in Massachusetts, Connecticut, or New Jersey.

Water that is moving quickly and being diverted by an obstruction, such as a point, a sandbar, an oyster bar, big rocks, or bridge pilings, will almost always hold the bigger fish in the river. Big bass that are living and feeding in a river are not any different than their brothers and sisters in the open ocean. They are searching for food and places to rest that also provide protection and comfort. The bigger fish use the channel's deeper water to travel effortlessly to and from the mouth of the river as well as to shallow-water areas.

All rivers have at least one deep side where the flow of the water has eroded the bank and the bottom over time and flushed the sand and silt downriver and out into the bay. Deep cuts and holes close to any structure are excellent big-fish areas, and you should investigate and fish them thoroughly.

Captain Joe Pagano of Stuff-It Charters holding a 50-pound striper taken in shallow water while tossing live eels at night into the rocks. Pagano is an expert at fishing shallow-water for big fish after dark.

Any bridge that spans a river will also be a good area to fish. However, if there is more than one bridge, you better check both of them as one might have more to offer than the other depending on its location. You also need to fish a bridge throughout all stages of the tide to find at which point the fish are feeding. The bite around a bridge may only last for 15 or 20 minutes. High and low slack tides are often good times to target bridges. Abutments and corners will break the current and cause eddies to form where bass will lie next to and feed. Shadow lines are also likely targets for your lure.

Piers and bridges inside a river system that are lighted at night will hold baitfish beneath or near them.

As the tide rises and approaches high water, stripers will move close to shore near the spartina or eel grass in search of food. If the river has a viable run of alewives, that is the best scenario of all. On mornings or evenings when the water is calm, watch for the stripers' backs sticking out of the water or wakes caused by the fish pushing water. These fish

Disturbance in shallow water may provide a clue to a striper's location.

can be finicky and hard to get to hit a lure or fly, so you'll need a lot of patience. This is when a fly rod can be effective, as its delicate presentation is less likely to spook the fish, and, in able hands, it allows for precise casts.

A few other things to look for in calm water are swirls, tail fins, or other signs of activity. Skipping or jumping baitfish are usually a good sign that there are feeding fish beneath them. Egrets, cormorants, and other fish-eating birds also indicate baitfish are in the area. Work these areas completely before you move on.

As you make your way up a river, be aware that this environment is usually quiet and tranquil, especially after dark. It's totally different from fishing a bay, big cove, or the open ocean. The less noise you create while moving or fishing, the more likely you will catch fish. Over the years, I've learned that a more subtle presentation works much better in calm conditions. Yet I consistently see guys tossing three-, four-, and five-ounce poppers in mirror-calm water, causing so much noise it could be bottled and used as a lighthouse warning system. Do they catch a fish here and there? Yes, but not nearly as consistently as they could be catching them. A big, noisy lure has its place on the ocean, where there is already a lot of noise, but not in the calmness of a river. The one exception might be the Zara Spook, a big surface lure that pushes water in front of it but doesn't really cause a lot of noise.

Bait, Flies, and Lures

During the summer when menhaden move into the rivers, live menhaden are first on my list of big-bass baits. Next would be live eels. Live eels are good because most rivers have populations of them. Fresh-cut bait is also effective, though I don't enjoy fishing that way. Alewives would be on the list, but currently possessing or using them is illegal in Rhode Island, Connecticut, and Massachusetts.

Now is the time for big flies. Herring and bunker flies as long as you can get them work well when the bass are on big bait. I like putting purple, yellow, olive, or pink tinges in them. The more neutral tones seem to get more strikes, but length and shape are by far the most important aspects of a good imitation. When fishing the shallows, you can use a floating or intermediate line. For deeper portions of the river, use a sinking line. Mix up your retrieve—some days the fish will prefer a fast retrieve and on others, a stop-and-go rhythm might be better. Big eel patterns that float or swim just under the surface also work well.

Big 9-inch Slug-Gos and 10-inch Fin-S Fish work great in a river loaded with good-size baitfish. They present large-profile baits with

Capt. Jim White fights a big bass close to the boat. This is where most good fish are lost or broken off, so you need to pay close attention to what you are doing, and what the fish is doing.

Dave Denda poses with a big striper that ate an eel during the day in a tidal river. On some days, neither lures nor flies will work, and the fish prefer fresh meat. I always try to have a few eels on board when fishing during the day—just in case.

little or no noise as they enter the water. Some other options are big plastic shad bodies, which now come in a size that rivals the real thing, some as long as 16 inches. Wooden swimming plugs like Tattoos, Dannys, and Atoms also work.

Night fishing is often slow in stained or muddy water. Clear water is more productive when fishing at night.

For fishing the deeper sections of the river, such as channels and bridge abutments, I like using 6- to 9-inch Ronz lures and weighted shad bodies like Storms, Calcuttas, and 6-inch Lunker City shads. You can get these lures deep to reach fish holding close to bottom structure.

CHAPTER 5

TIDES AND CURRENTS

TIDES AND CURRENTS, along with the books and charts that document them, are likely the least understood and least discussed aspects of fishing. This chapter covers the terminology and essential features of tides and currents important to fishermen and where to seek out more information on these topics. There is no substitute for time on the water, though.

Jigging the current produced this nice striper. In some areas, a strong current will run adjacent to shallow water, and the fish will hold close by.

Fishing in Currents

Most fish lie facing into the current, waiting for food to come to them. Waiting in this fashion gives them the stability they must have so they don't expend too much energy while feeding. That is one of the reasons why casting up-current or quartering across the flow, and not down-current, is most effective. Lures and flies that approach fish from behind just don't look natural. Bass will often seek out and hide behind structure such as boulders, sandbars, or wrecks (or anything else they can use), waiting to ambush their food.

Your tidal reference information will tell you how fast a current is moving throughout most stages of the tide and where big bass are most likely to be holding and resting when not feeding. When the current is moving at top speed, stripers will hold close to the bottom, as the current there is usually much slower than it is toward the surface. The current speed will also dictate what type and weight

Captain Jim White holds a nice bass for a client caught in a riverbed channel where the current was running strong.

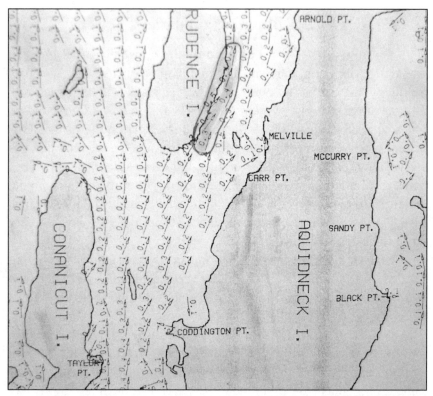

Current diagrams such as this one show you the best areas where the currents are strongest at all stages of the tides. Scour the resources of universities and government research agencies such as NOAA for this type of information.

of lure, or in the case of fly fishing, which type of fly line (floating, intermediate, sinking) you should use. In some of these areas it's important to get down quickly before your fly or lure swings out of the strike zone. Some areas of current go from deep to shallow in a matter of a few feet, so getting your lure or fly to come up from the bottom toward the top in a natural manner is critical to your presentation. In these instances, you may have to use a sinking line, weighted fly, or a heavier jighead. Tidal movement during the first and second quarter of the moon is less than at other periods. At these times, rivers, which already have natural current flow and can be hard to get your lure to the bottom, are easier to fish deeper.

Influences on Tides

High and low tides, labeled as AM and PM, are usually listed for each day, along with the tide height. The moon and sun have a great impact on tides. The sun has an effect on tides because of its huge mass (26 million times that of the moon), whereas the moon is four-hundred times closer to the earth than the sun, so its effect on the earth is estimated to be 2.17 times more than that of the sun. The moon's phase is always the most important factor affecting ocean tides. The difference between high and low tide is greatest during the full and new moon, and these two stages will also force more water than usual into an area. Also, tides will be at their highest when the moon is closest to the center of the earth (perigree).

The effect of the moon's declination can also cause tides of different heights on the same day. This can be very perplexing to anglers who go to an area expecting a certain tidal stage and find that the water is either higher or lower. Blame it on the moon.

Wind also affects tides. During high tide, especially under a full or new moon, a strong wind blowing in the same direction as the tide will tend to raise the height of the tide. When a strong wind pushes in the same direction as a dropping tide, the water will be much lower than normal.

Fishing the Full Moon

It has long been said that the best fishing will occur for three days prior and three days after the full moon. I suppose that in some cases this may be true, but in my experience, as well as that of others, the day before, the day of, and the day after the full moon are close to being a waste of time. If that time period is accompanied by strong winds blowing in the same direction as the tide, it will probably be even worse. The big tides that accompany the full moon pull an awful lot of debris and weeds into the water, making shallow-water areas difficult to fish.

In areas with big tidal fluctuations, like Boston and points north, the effects of the full moon may not be as great, as the fish are used to dealing with these fluctuations in the first place. In areas where the tidal rise and fall is minimal, such as two to four feet, the balance of nature is upset when five, six, or seven feet of water moves into areas that aren't normally used to having that much in the system. I can't speak for every area of the coast, but in Rhode Island, the arrival of big water usually shuts good fishing spots down tight as a drum. Fish will also tend to feed more at night when the moon is full and lie low during the day. I much prefer to fish the first quarter, third quarter, and dark of the moon (new moon).

Many surf fishermen that I have asked feel the same way. They say that a full moon can be good until it gets to about ten o'clock in the sky, and then it becomes too high and lights the water too much. Some full-moon nights are so bright that you can see almost as clearly as during the day. When this occurs, it's like someone throws a switch, and the fish shut down. Once the moon gets back to around three o'clock in the sky, they say the fish will once again begin to feed.

The farther you go up a bay or a big river the narrower the land around it usually becomes. This bottleneck can cause the water to pick up speed as water behind it pushes toward shore. Where rivers enter a bay, their mouths will likely have the strongest tides, and the farther you go upriver toward its headwaters, the tides will begin to weaken as the amount of fresh water coming down from above mixes with the salt water and slows its speed. At the very top end of a river system there will be little or no tidal movement. Breachways, bends in the river, deep channels next to shallow water, or man-made obstructions also affect the strength of tides and can harbor fish at different stages of the tide.

Charts and Books

One of the first things you can do to increase your chances of finding big-fish holding areas is to obtain quality charts of the areas you intend to fish, as well as a good tide and current table book. The *Eldridge Tide and Pilot Book* is one of the best sources of information you can have on your boat or in your truck. It is also inexpensive. It includes listings of current tables, daily high- and low-water tables, and weather and navigational data.

PERSONAL LOGBOOK

A collection of my logbooks for four years. Logbooks help you keep track of past conditions and patterns. Fill them out completely and with as much information as possible. After a few seasons, you'll be surprised at how much valuable information you have gathered.

One of the best ways to keep track of fishing information is to keep a logbook with notes on relevant information for every trip such as date, time of day, tides, wind speed and direction, moon phase, and water conditions, clarity, and temperature. Over time, this will become a valuable aid in understanding how all these factors play a vital role in how fish react to varying conditions and stages of the tide. A clear picture will emerge, and you will know just where and when you need to be in a particular area for the best action. Striped bass are predictable. After forty years on the water, I still find big fish in the same places and at the same times and tidal stages as I did in the beginning. Not only that, but they are still feeding at the same stages of the tide.

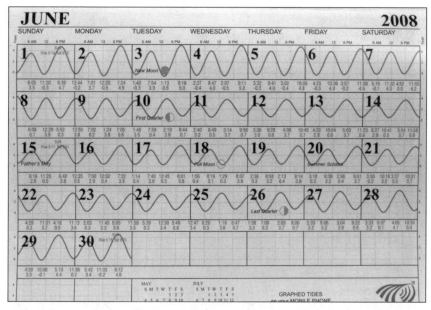

Tide chart calendars, or just simple tide charts, are essential. You can't be fishing at the right time if you don't know when and what the tide is doing.

The two parts of most interest are the tide and current tables. They will tell you when you should be at your favorite spot to catch fish. Fishing highly productive areas at the right time of the tide and when the current is moving best are crucial to finding and catching big fish. Since striped bass are creatures of current as well as tides, it's nearly impossible to catch the bigger fish without understanding these two key factors. Big stripers hunt and capture baitfish that are trapped in the turmoil of a strong rip or the swiftness of the current and are struggling to escape. You can also check with your local university to see if they have up-to-date current flow charts for your area. These charts usually include the current's strength, direction of flow, when and where one or more currents meet, and duration of current.

Reed's Nautical Logbook is two to three times as thick as the Eldridge book and twice the price. Its tide and current tables are said to be accepted by the U.S. Coast Guard as a lot more accurate than those in the Eldridge book. I've used both and haven't found any difference except that Reed's has more information.

These keys on charts explain the symbols on a nautical chart. Study them so you know what they refer to. Many of the same symbols are used on GPS maps as well.

You will also need an accurate and up-to-date NOAA nautical navigation chart of the area that you are going to fish. A good chart will give you a clearer picture of the underwater world and pinpoint areas for you to investigate. Some companies offer three-dimensional charts for your computer that depict the bottom contours and features with amazing detail, which you can lay over NOAA charts or interface with your home computer and GPS system for optimal accuracy. Along with a NOAA chart, you should also have *The Nautical Chart/Symbols and Abbreviations, Chart No. 1*, which explains all the markings and confusing symbols that accompany nautical charts. Every chart published by NOAA has a chart key that explains all of the symbols on the chart. This will show you the chart's scale, bottom makeup, and the location of rocks, wrecks, channels, bars, and sand flats.

Acquiring these tools and taking the time to understand them will tip the odds greatly in your favor, rather than just going out blindly, as so many anglers choose to do. The more questions that you can answer and problems you can solve before arriving on the water, the more and bigger fish you will likely begin to catch on a consistent basis.

NOAA Terminology

We'll begin with some terminology and definitions associated with tides and current. I follow each of my brief and much-simplified explanations with the definitions the National Oceanographic and Atmospheric Administration (NOAA) uses when referring to charts, tables, and tidal information.

Current

In everyday terms, current is the movement of the water up and down, from high to low tide and then back again. Nontidal current are those that are always moving in the oceans from one place to another, and the rise and fall of the tides has little or no effect on them.

> **NOAA:** Current is the horizontal movement of water. Tidal currents are caused by the gravitational movements between the sun, the moon, and the earth and are a part of the same general movements

Fishing when the tides are at their optimum will account for a lot of nice bass like this one. Not all tides will produce fish, so it's up to you to figure out which ones are the best in the area you fish.

of the sea that is manifested in the vertical rise and fall called tide. Nontidal currents include the permanent currents in the general circulation system of the sea, as well as temporary currents arising from more pronounced meteorological variability.

Ebb Current

Ebb current is when the tide is moving out or falling, going from high to low. The greater and lesser ebb refers to the speed of the current before it actually stops on the bottom of the tide known as slack tide.

NOAA: Ebb current is the movement of tidal current away from the shore or down a tidal river or estuary. In the mixed type of reversing tidal current, the terms "greater ebb" and "lesser ebb" are used respectively to refer to the ebb tidal currents of the greater and lesser speed of each day. The terms "maximum ebb" and "minimum ebb" are applied to the maximum and minimum speeds of a current running continuously at ebb, the speed alternately increasing and decreasing without coming to a slack or reversing movement. The expression maximum ebb is also applicable to any ebb current at the time of its greatest speed.

Stripers will lie facing into a current.

Flood Current

Flood current is the tide moving in toward shore or land and is often referred to as incoming tide. Minimum and maximum refer to its speed before it tops out at high slack water.

NOAA: Flood current is the movement of a tidal current toward the shore or up a tidal river or an estuary. In the mixed type of reversing current, the terms "greater flood" and "lesser flood" are applied respectively to the flood currents of greater and lesser speeds of each day. The terms "maximum flood" and "minimum flood" are used to describe the maximum and minimum speeds of a flood current, the speed of which alternately increases and decreases without coming to a slack or reversing movement. The expression maximum flood is also applicable to any flood current at the time of its greatest speed.

High Tide (High Water)

High tide is when the tide has reached it maximum height and stops. New and full moons can change the time of high tide due to the extra water they bring into any water system. The scientists at NOAA don't like the term "high tide," preferring "high water" instead, but high tide is what everyone uses and has used for as long as I can remember.

> NOAA: High water (HW) is the maximum height reached by a rising tide. The height may be due solely to the periodic tidal forces, or it may have superimposed upon it the effects of prevailing meteorological conditions. Use of the synonymous term "high tide," is discouraged.

Low Tide (Low Water)

Low tide, also called low water, is when the water has reached its lowest point. As with high tides, the new and full moons will change the times that the tides reach their lowest point.

These two anglers have located a school of stripers that were moving just off the beach during the fall. Just outside of the wash line, beaches hold some nice size stripers.

NOAA: Low water (LW) is the minimum height reached by a falling tide. The height may be due solely to the periodic tidal forces, or it may have superimposed upon it the effects of meteorological conditions. Use of the synonymous term "low tide" is discouraged.

Neap Tides

Neap tides occur during the quarter moons and are not as strong as spring tides, nor do they last as long.

NOAA: Neap tides are tides of decreased range or tidal currents of decreased speed occurring semimonthly as the result of the moon being in quadrature (i.e., when it has an angular separation of ninety degrees from the sun, as seen from the earth). The "neap range" (Np) of the tide is the average semidiurnal range occurring at the time of neap tides and is most conveniently computed from the harmonic constants. It is smaller than the mean range where the type of tide is either semidiurnal or missed and is of no practical significance where the type of tide is diurnal. The average height of the high waters of the neap tides is called "neap high water" or "high water neaps" (MHWN), and the average height of the corresponding low waters is called "neap low water" or "low water neaps" (MLWN).

Spend more time on the flats during neap tides and not spring tides. Spring tides tend to dump more water off the flat, exposing more sand and mud, and the fish won't stay as long.

Spring Tides

Spring tides are the strongest tides of the season and occur during the full and new moons. At this time (usually in June and September where I fish), the tides are higher and lower than usual.

NOAA: Spring tides are tides of increased range or tidal currents of increased speed occurring semimonthly as the result of the moon being new or full. The "spring range" (Sg) of the tide is the average

Captain Ryan Sansoucy specializes in locating big stripers in shallow water for his fly-fishing clients. Ryan uses a flats boat to get into skinny water and sight-cast to big cruising fish.

semidiurnal range occurring at the time of spring tides and is most conveniently computed from the harmonic constants. It is larger than the mean range where the type of tide is either semi-diurnal or mixed, and is of no practical significance where the type of tide is diurnal. The mean of the high waters of the spring tide is called spring high water or mean high wa-

River fish are very tide-sensitive. When you fish a tidal river and the fish stop biting, it's usually time to move. If the tide is dropping, go downriver; if it's rising, move upriver to intercept the fish.

ter springs (MHWS), and the average height of the corresponding low waters is called spring low water or mean low water springs (MLWS).

Tidal Current Tables

This is your basic tide chart that you see in magazines, newspapers, and other publications. It usually gives you the time and range (in feet) of the daily highs and lows for each day of the month.

NOAA: Tide current tables give daily predictions of the times and speeds of the tidal currents. Current differences and constants through which additional predictions can be obtained for numerous other places usually supplement these predictions.

Tide

Tide is the rise and fall of water each day.

NOAA: Tide is the periodic rise and fall of the water resulting from the gravitational interactions between the sun, moon, and earth. Also, the vertical component of the particulate motion of a tidal wave. Although the accompanying horizontal movement of the water is part of the same phenomenon, it is preferable to designate this motion as "tidal current."

Tide Tables

Tide tables are tabulated to reflect the averages of the highs and lows over a period of time. They will include the high of the water for low and high tide as well as time differences, especially for areas within a bay or river system, where the high and low tides may be earlier or later than on the open ocean.

Strong winds will cloud and silt shallow water first and deeper water later. Fish will hang in this transition zone between the clean and cloudy water.

NOAA: Tables that give the daily predictions of the times and heights of high and low waters. These predictions are usually supplemented by tidal differences and constants through which additional predictions can be obtained for numerous other places.

CHAPTER 6

UNDER THE COVER OF DARKNESS: A BIG FISH TALE

MANY OF THE BIG FISH I've caught over the years have been after the sun went down on dark, moonless nights. Of eight fish over 50 pounds, and one that went 60, five were taken during the night. Night offers many advantages when trying to fool large stripers. The first advantage is concealment. It is much harder for the fish to notice your presence when it's pitch black. Second, the bigger fish are generally more likely to be active at night and looking to feed in the fertile shallow water.

But just because it's dark, there is no guarantee you'll catch fish. For instance, when there is an abundance of adult menhaden in an area, night fishing can often take a dive. The bigger fish will feed during the day and take it easy after dark. When big baits like bunker are scarce or nowhere to be found, the bite will usually return to the night-time hours, especially during the summer and early fall.

A beautiful striped bass taken in the wash on a dark night. Notice the angler's head lamp so he can see when it's necessary. Use light sparingly at night, as others in the area will not take kindly to you turning it on all the time.

For night fishing to be productive, the conditions need to be right, and you need to be in the right place at the right time. But, how do you know when and where to go? As I think back on the fish I've taken or have seen caught at night, there are a lot of examples that I could describe for you. However, the example that may best illustrate the importance of picking the right spot occurred on June 12, 2007. On that cold, windy, rainy evening, we put our first sixty-pound striper aboard *White Ghost 2*, as well as two in the fifties, three in the forties, and one that went thirty-nine—all on the same night. It had been decades since I'd experienced that type of fishing, but it was those thousands of hours on the water that helped me determine where we should go on that particular night. And the payoff was huge.

The Tale Begins

Earlier the previous morning I had taken clients out on a five-hour trip and had good success fishing with live menhaden, boating four or five bass over 20 pounds and two over 30 pounds. The fishing had been so good that I didn't want to miss one minute of it, as you never know if or when you'll see fishing like that again. At noon I called my good friend, Billy "Eel Man" Nolan, whom I've since renamed "Billy Bunker." I asked him if he would like to go fishing the next morning, since I was free and didn't have a charter the next day. Billy quickly agreed, and we met at my marina late that afternoon to get things ready and grab some fresh bait so we could leave early in the morning without having to stop.

While on my boat tying rigs, Billy and I were discussing the recent barrage of big fish that had entered our bay, the likes of which no one had seen in almost thirty years or more, as well as how terrific the fishing had been thus far this early in the season. Billy had taken a 47 and a 51-pounder just the week before, and this was his first full year fishing from a boat rather than from shore.

As we talked, I had the marine weather channel on VHF, listening for the following day's forecast. It wasn't encouraging. The forecast called for winds from 15 to 20

Dave Denda struggles with a big bass when he grabs him boatside during the night. Once you decide to grab hold of a big fish, hold on tightly. I usually wear a glove to get a better grip on the fish.

mph, gusting to 25, with accompanying rain. Not quite the type of conditions you'd like to go out and fish in, but it was what it was, and there wasn't anything we could do about it. As we listened to weather predictions we didn't want to hear, I kept thinking in the back of my mind about what two old gents had told me about such conditions many years ago when I had just returned home from military service.

A surf caster needs to wade slowly and cautiously when entering the water, especially when the sun is going down.

Wisdom from the Old Pros

I had met the two when I was twenty-three years old and fresh out of the Army. The only thing I wanted to do after three years of military service was to fish until I dropped, so I decided to try my hand at commercial rod-and-reel fishing, which a couple of friends had been doing, as well as clamming and running some lobster traps. I was willing to do just about anything to make some money, so long as it was on the water and did not involve punching a time clock at some nine-to-five job. Not that there's anything wrong with that, but it just wasn't my thing at the time.

One afternoon I pulled into the dock at the same time as two old gents. After tying up their 20-footer to the dock, they asked me how I had done during the morning tide. I answered with some embarrassment, as my eyes were fixated on the huge pile of fish they were tossing on the dock, whereas I had only caught two of about 20 pounds or so. I quickly found out that we had both been using the same bait, live river herring, so these two guys really had tied my shorts in knots and handed them back to me.

For whatever reason—pity, I suppose—one looked at the other and then said, "Come 'ere kid." I walked down the dock toward them, oozing with excitement as to what I might be told. Both of these old gents were known throughout the bay system as high hooks who rarely came back to the dock empty-handed. Keep in mind that we're talking about the days when fishing information was not given out freely to anyone, if given at all. Guys would lie to their own friends and brothers to keep a spot secret. Having the opportunity to gain some inside information, especially from these two, was akin to hitting the lottery four times in the same day.

The one old gent then asked me, "Do you know why you only caught two fish, kid?"

"No, I guess I really don't know," I answered.

"Well, you were about four hours too late and pretty close to ten miles from where the fish are at this time of year," he advised me.

At this point I felt almost useless and certainly depressed at my inability to make a big haul in a bay that was currently full of huge stripers. But the one thing I hadn't counted on was that these two old guys had taken notice of my effort and dedication at this game, fish or no fish. I was there day in and day out, in all types of weather and sea conditions.

"Listen here kid," one said. "George and I like you. We see you here every morning going out and working your ass off out here no matter what the weather. Granted, you don't do so well, but we like your moxie," he said.

Moxie? What the hell is that? Must be something from that older generation. I was thinking I'd just been insulted by the two guys I admired the most.

"We're gonna turn you on to a spot we know and see how you handle it. Keep it to yourself, keep your mouth shut, and we just might give you some others. Open your mouth to anyone about what we tell you, and you'll never catch more than those two fish you got there today."

His warning was taken to heart. What they didn't know is that I had been raised and trained to keep my mouth shut about fishing spots. My grandfather and my father were of Portuguese descent, and were also fishermen. From the time I was old enough to walk or remember, it had been drilled into my hard skull: You tell no one anything, period! You didn't even want to consider the consequences if you broke that rule.

The old gents then told me that when a northeast blow approaches and it coincides with an evening tide that's going to drop just after dark during the month of June, and it's close to the new moon, head to Bull Rock Point and fish it hard. (Obviously, the name of the spot is fictitious. I don't want my grandfather or my old man coming back to whack me upside the head for divulging where we were really fishing. I guess I'm just superstitious.)

"You'll see a rip form from the wind and the dropping tide as it's being pushed out by the northeast wind, right along the west side of the shoreline. The only time that you will see that rip form is when those conditions all come together. Otherwise, the area is barren and looks totally fishless and mostly never holds anything but a few schoolies. But when those conditions are in place, the fish stack up there along that rip and you can really hammer them all night long."

Over the ensuing years, they were proven right over and over. I took hundreds upon hundreds of fish from that area, all during the night, and always during those conditions they described.

Bull Rock Point

I related this story to Billy while we were rigging hooks and cleaning up. I told him I hadn't been to Bull Rock Point in quite a few years, mainly because there really hadn't been all that many big bass in our bay in recent times and the effort just wasn't worth it. We now had thousands upon thousands of adult menhaden swimming around in our bay, and the fish were coming inside from everywhere to chow down on them, just like they had thirty years prior. It was so good that a guy we met one morning while we were snagging our bait said, "Welcome to 1974."

After a minute or two of mulling it over, we decided to go for it. After all, what did we have to lose? We donned our rain gear, prepared the boat, and made sure all was secure. We then stopped to snag some menhaden, put about twenty or so in the live well, and headed to Bull Rock Point. The ride over there was sloppy, wet, and cold, and the forecast

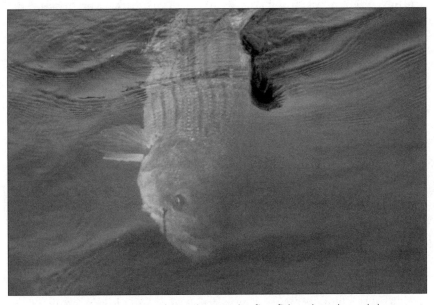

A big bass comes alongside *White Ghost 2*, the first fish to be released that evening. If you are going to release the fish, grab it by the mouth, with a Boga Grip, or a big net.

was for more wind and rain. It got so miserable, that about halfway there, we considered turning back to the marina. But, urged on by curiosity and the lure of big bass, we continued on.

Upon arriving, we slowly approached the shoreline and got in close. When we were in about 5 or 6 feet of water, we dropped the anchor and let out enough rope so we were right next to the drop-off, where the water fell to 15 feet. Like magic, the rip began to form as we watched wide-eyed in amazement. Here we were, thirty years later, and it was exactly the same as the first time I had laid eyes on it. Billy was beside himself. "I really didn't believe you," he said later.

Hogs

Billy grabbed a pogy, hooked it through the nose, and sent it flying into the wind and rain. I did the same on the opposite side of the boat. About five minutes or so went by when Billy's rod went off. He grabbed it from the gunwale rod holder, counted to six, and set the hook hard, sending a whoosh through the wind and rain. After a brief battle we placed the fish on the Boga Grip, and she pulled 47 pounds. Not a bad way to start the evening. But it had only just begun.

As we were taking some photos, my rod got hit. I quickly put down the camera, grabbed my stick, and set the hook. When my rod bent in two and my drag began to scream, Billy remarked, "Hey, I think you got a good one."

"I think so too," I replied.

Ten minutes later, Billy dragged her over the side of the gunwale, and we both said, "Wow!" Once again the big Boga came out. I held it up and Billy read the scale. "She's fifty-four," he said. While this was happening, Billy kept repeating to himself, "This is amazing! This is amazing! I can't believe this!" At least I believe he was talking to himself, as it didn't seem like he was addressing me.

We re-baited and tossed two more menhaden back out. The rain was now coming down much harder, and whitecaps were visible out in the middle of the bay, despite the darkness. It was a good thing we were anchored in close and protected by the bend in the land, but it was getting nasty in a hurry. Billy then asked me if I thought that we should stick it out or go back in. I quickly replied, "Are you kidding me? A forty-seven and a fifty-four in less than ten minutes? We're going to stay here until tomorrow morning, if necessary. We got plenty of coffee, food, cigars, and cigarettes. No need to go anywhere but right here."

I then lit a cigar and Billy lit a cigarette. Billy couldn't have taken two drags when his rod once again went off. This time the fish weighed 41 pounds. I followed a few minutes later with another 50-pounder. There goes a good cigar.

Billy "Eel Man" Nolan sits to rest after landing a 51-pound striper, the first of two 50-pounders that evening. Not all nights are like this, of course, but learning when to be there at the right time can lead to the fish of a lifetime.

After what seemed like seconds (it was probably more like five or so minutes), Billy's rod goes off once more. I watch him wait patiently. He waits, lets the line tighten down, and then strikes hard. Immediately his drag engages, and the line flows off the reel like a hot knife through butter.

"Jimmy!" he says. "This is a big fish, and she's heading for the shoreline and that rock pile over there."

I turn on the spreader lights on the tower to get a better idea of where the fish is heading, but the rain is now coming in sheets, so even with the lights on it's hard to see. I then notice his line ticking and say, "What's going on with your line? Why is it bouncing like that?"

"She's bouncing off of the rocks," Billy explains. "I can feel it. I'm never going to land this fish. No way," he says nervously.

The fish decides to head out and go deep. After ten or twelve minutes, she's now close to coming alongside, and we get our first look at her. We are both shocked at what we see. The fish is much bigger than the 50-pounder we had boated. I went for the gaff, not wanting to chance missing her with the Boga Grip. Yes, we gaffed her. A lot of people complained when they heard that, but I defy anyone who sees a fish of this size coming alongside their boat not to go for the gaff and risk losing the fish. My Boga Grip only went to 60 pounds, and that hog pulled it right to the bottom.

"How big do you think she is?" Billy asked.

"I don't know for sure, but I'd say you got yourself a sixty, kid." I answered.

"How are we going to weigh it?" he said.

"We'll have to take it to the shop when we get in." (I was working at Quaker Lane Bait and Tackle at the time.)

"But the shop is closed," Billy said.

"I got the keys. We can use the big digital scale that we weigh the deer on for the state," I assured him.

Over the next hour, we land another 50-pounder, two over 40 pounds, and two over 30 pounds. We then pulled the anchor and headed for home. It was a long, wet, rough ride, but we had struck gold. We had hit the mother lode of big bass, and we'd been fishing in only 6 to 7 feet of water.

At the shop at 1 A.M., the fish pulled 60 pounds, 4 ounces on the big digital scale. This was the fish of a lifetime; the culmination of literally tens of thousands of hours—fishing, searching, learning, testing, and taking beatings from the sea.

After, the rumors flew. Guys were telling *me* how and where we caught the fish. There were even rumors that we got it from a gill net-ter—the stories were endless. I later told one guy we shot it with a .40 caliber H&K automatic. It bordered on the absurd, as everyone tried to figure out how, when, and where we'd landed those fish. Did we use cut-up pogies or live ones? Did we anchor or drift? Did we cast or troll? The only thing we'd confirm is that Billy got his first 60-pound fish. And the only other ones who know for sure saw it happen from heaven on a windy, rainy, June night in a northeast blow.

Lessons

Now you may ask, what's the point to this long story, other than that we caught some big fish on a rainy, windy night? The point is that there's more to catching big fish than just fishing after dark. Not only was it dark, but we had the correct wind accompanying the correct tide with the arrival of a low-pressure system; we had the proper bait; and we were where the fish were on that particular night.

That wasn't the only spot to fish well that evening. Two days later we spoke with friends of ours who had also gone out that evening and who had also been successful. Two of them were fishing from the surf and the other from a boat. They had been working areas where they knew fish would be, given those conditions.

We could have taken the easy way out and gone home and went to bed and waited for the next morning. It might have been just as good, but then again, it might not have. By morning the bite might have already been finished. Both Billy and I had fished until almost noon on the day before our nighttime trip—he by himself, and me with clients. But we both chose to push ourselves and deal with the conditions. There are no magic solutions, no special tricks or tactics, no magic-bait answers to being successful. Time on the water is the only solution.

CHAPTER 7

BIG LURES, BIG FISH

L ARGER STRIPERS ARE LAZY BY NATURE, and they got big by
not being stupid or overly aggressive when it comes to feeding.
Though they will take smaller lures and flies when the predominate
bait is small, their survival skills have shown them that eating one
big meal such as a menhaden, river herring, large squid, or mackerel
is much more efficient than eating lots of smaller stuff. It's also safer.
And they will always pick the safest, easiest, and fastest way to eat, as
well as being extremely cautious before committing themselves to the
attack. If that weren't true, everyone would be catching big fish all the
time.

When you look back at the history of big fish and what they were
caught on; you'll see a definite pattern of big bait, big fish. The record
books are loaded with entries of big stripers being caught on big swimmers, large poppers, four-foot-long tube lures, and big live baits. Once
again, I am speaking of averages here. There is no such thing as *for
certain* in monster bass fishing, except that the sun will rise and set and
the tide rise and fall.

Once you decide to make the switch to larger lures, you will reduce
the numbers of fish that you are going to catch. Although you will still

catch a fair number of smaller fish on these bigger lures (I've never seen bait so big that a striper of any size won't try and eat it if he has a mind to), it will be far less than if you were tossing small- to medium-size plugs. That's just a fact of life. Targeting big fish means giving up lots of smaller ones. A lot of guys don't take the time and effort required to target big fish and stick with it until they are successful.

I only carry fifteen or so different types of lures on my boat. There is a good reason for this. You get to know exactly what each lure does and under what conditions it will be effective. It's a lot better to fish fewer lures extremely well than trying to fish dozens of lures and changing them all the time. It's also better to have a smaller selection of colors, styles, and actions than a boatful of lures, many of which will never see the water. Learn to fish proven lures efficiently and effectively, and you'll catch more and bigger fish on a fairly consistent basis

Capt. Jim Misto took this nice bass on a yellow Tattoo Surface Swimmer early in the morning in shallow water. Yellow plugs and flies work very well on cloudy and overcast days as well as early in the morning. Tattoo's Tackle makes one of the best surface swimmers out there today.

Always target structure (whether it is visible or not) when fishing any type of lure. Cast near the front, to the sides, and behind things such as rocks and reefs along the shoreline. If you can't see the structure, look for white water, which signals structure below. Cast into the white-water wash and on all sides of it.

Big Plugs

The number of finely crafted custom plugs has grown by leaps and bounds in the past ten years alone, not counting models that have been introduced by the big lure manufacturers. To cover them all would be impossible. In this chapter, I focus on those lures that have brought me repeated success for many years, and I apologize in advance to those manufacturers I leave out because of space limitations.

Swimmers

Swimmers are one of the oldest types of lures and still one of the most common, as they imitate a type of food—swimming baitfish—that make up the biggest portion of the diets of most gamefish. Stick with the basic colors—white, yellow, black, chartreuse, and green.

Tattoo Swimmer. My number-one go-to swimmer now is Tattoo's two-ounce surface swimmer. Custom-made in Rhode Island, it's one of the newer generations of swimmers that have captured the wiggle and roll of Danny Pichney's famous Danny Swimmer line (see below), now manufactured by Gibbs Lures, also in Rhode Island. The Tattoo Surface Swimmer has re-created that rock-and-roll to perfection and has a special ability to raise fish under tough conditions, such as daylight and when the area is loaded with adult menhaden. I've had the most success with white, yellow, black, and bunker.

Atom 40. This classic swimmer was born in the late 1940s and is still catching fish today. It is now being made by the Uncle Josh Bait Company, which purchased the rights to its production. The blue and white, the all-white, and the orange and yellow are still some of the best color combos ever produced for catching big bass.

Danny Swimmers. If you already own some original Danny Swimmers, cherish them. They are classic big-bass baits. Today, the Danny-

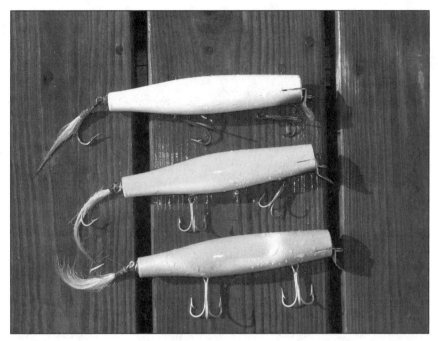

A selection of Danny Swimmers by the late Danny Pichney. These lures are now manufactured by Gibbs Lures of Cumberland, Rhode Island, and still account for their fair share of fish. The original Danny Swimmer was said to be almost as good as live bait at times.

style swimmer is being made by Gibbs Lure Company. The short, 1¼-ounce swimmer can be deadly on all sizes of stripers, and it also comes in a 6-inch model. Reel it in slowly so you get that enticing V wake on the surface of the water. The closer to the surface you can fish this lure, the better it will produce for you.

Creek Chub Pikie. The original Creek Chub Pikie swimmer is back, in 8- and 12-inch (jointed) versions. The 8-inch model is offered in wood as well as plastic. Since their re-introduction two years ago, they have already accounted for a lot of big stripers on my boat. You can fish these lures on or just below the surface, depending on water conditions. The newer versions maintain the Pikie's unique action. An interesting piece of history regarding this lure is that the Pikie Swimmer was the model used by Bob Pond to create his famous Atom Swim-

A nice big bass nailed this Tattoo Swimmer worked over some shallow-water reefs along a shoreline during the spring. A good heavy-action rod and 20-pound-test mono is required to get a good hook-set on fish this size when fishing big lures.

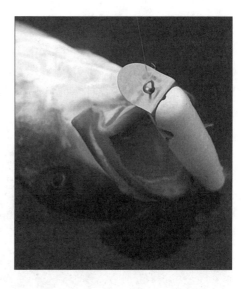

mer back in the 1940s when he found a Pikie stuck in a rock in the Cape Cod Canal.

Cotton Cordell Red Fin. A lure forgotten by many, but still a big-fish catcher, the big Red Fin's unique wiggle draws big stripers out of hiding. Replacing the rear treble hook with a single Siwash salmon hook (open-eye) dressed with bucktail or feathers makes it even more effective. The Red Fin has long been a favorite for stripers in large freshwater impoundments.

Bomber Magnum. Sometimes you need a lure that gets just a bit deeper, even in shallow water. Straight and jointed Bomber Magnums are excellent choices in areas where sandbars, rock piles, shelves, or ridges drop from 2 or 3 feet to 6 to 10 feet. It's also built to withstand and hold big fish, and now comes in a saltwater series. Bomber Swimmers are also a good choice when fishing in currents as they handle the faster water very well.

Rapala Super Shad Rap. This lure is 5½ inches long and is a good imitation of a bunker or river herring. Its wide body profile can be fished on, near, or just below the surface, and it has super-strong VMC hooks. The slower you reel this lure in, the better it will work for you.

Rapala Magnum. When you leave the United States to go fishing, the one line of lures that you find, even in the remotest of areas, are Rapalas. What can be said about the 7-inch Magnum that hasn't already been written? After fifty years it's still catching big fish. It can be fished slowly across the surface or fished with a quick jerk retrieve

A white Tattoo Surface Swimmer with a bucktail teaser is one of the finest wooden swimmers being made today. It has the ability to draw big fish from down below to the surface, even during the day.

as a twitch-bait just below the surface, depending on how the fish are feeding at the time.

Yo-Zuri Squid. Designed as a trolling lure, this extremely realistic squid imitation is deadly on big bass when the squid are running. We use a floating crankbait-style retrieve. Cast it out, crank it down one to three feet, allow it to float back toward the surface, and then repeat the process.

Yo-Zuri Crystal Minnow. The Crystal Minnow has one of the finest finishes on the market today. With lots of light reflection from its "crystal" body finish, it works great when the water is roiled or off-color. It floats, so you can fish it in many shallow-water areas without getting hung up all the time. Cast it out toward shore, let it rest, and then jerk it beneath the water with two or three jerks of the rod tip. This will cause the bait to dive down deeper. When you stop jerking, the bait will then rise up slowly toward the surface. Repeat this process until you've retrieved the lure back to the boat.

The reliable 7-inch Red Fin swimmer can still work its magic. Its slow side-to-side motion and distinctive V wake on the surface can draw big fish. Enhance its effectiveness by adding a single hook dressed with bucktail on the end.

Poppers

The sight and sound of a big striper attacking a popper in shallow water makes memories. Poppers or floating surf lures can cruise over obstructions such as rocks and reefs, whereas sinking plugs can quickly become stuck on rocks and other obstructions. With the price of lures today, that can get pretty expensive.

I like to use the **Smack-It Popper** when I need a surface lure with loud built-in rattles and heavy-duty hooks. The **Super Strike Popper** is tough, strong, and casts like a bullet. The white Super Strike has taken seven stripers over 35 pounds on our boat in the last three years and one over 40. I like to put a single hook on the rear and dress it with bucktail or feathers. Other poppers that I have used for a long time are the **Yo-Zuri Hydro Popper**, the **Gibbs Bottle Popper**, the **Rapala Skitter Popper**, and the **Creek Chub Striper Strike**. Fish poppers as slowly as possible when trying to entice big stripers.

Walkers

These lures all resemble the original dog-walker style **Zara Spook** that has been around for many years. The Zara Spook can draw fish from as

An assortment of big swimmers will fool big bass feeding on big bait such as menhaden, herring, or mackerel. The best colors are all-white, all-black, all-yellow, blue and white, and green and white.

These old-time swimmers are still producing fish today and show that you don't need hundreds of lures to catch fish, just ones that work and ones that you have confidence in.

deep as 30 feet or more when fished on a calm surface right above underwater structure. A walker's side-to-side, gliding action can prompt strikes in many different types of situations. They are also fun to fish. The category includes the **Yo-Zuri Surface Cruiser**, **Zara Spook Magnum** and **Super Magnum**, **Gibbs Pencil Popper**, and **Rapala X-Walker**. The differences between them are slight. All are long and slender and have that classic side-to-side motion. All have built-in rattle chambers, except for the Gibbs Pencil Popper. Even the new Super Magnum Zara Spook, now available in wood, has built-in rattles. While the Zara Spook and X-Walker don't pop when retrieved, they do splash on the surface. The Gibbs Pencil Popper is best fished with a fast whipping of the rod tip to make it dance and hop, which can be tiring after a while—but effective.

Needlefish Lures

Needlefish lures are simply pieces of wood or plastic shaped like a pencil with hooks, but they are some of the most effective lures ever made. The three most popular needlefish lures are **Hab's Needlefish**,

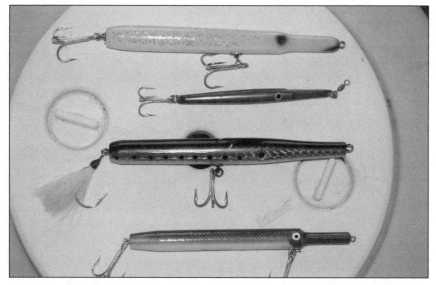

Needlefish lures work great on big stripers, even though they look simply ridiculous. Fish them slow, and when you think you are fishing them slow enough, slow down even more.

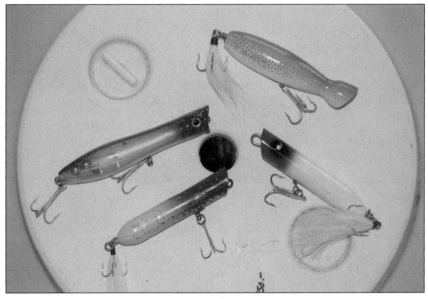

There is nothing like seeing a big striper demolish a surface popper in calm, shallow water. The adrenaline rush is simply incredible. Nothing hits a popper quite like a big striper. The Atom, Tsunami, Gibbs, and Creek Chub poppers are some of the favorites of boat and surf anglers.

Super Strike Needlefish, and **Gibbs Needlefish**. The Hab's and Gibbs are turned from wood, and the Super Strike is plastic. John Haberek passed away in 2007 at too young an age. He made one of the finest needlefish on the market, and his painted finishes were legendary. John was a good friend and an excellent fisherman, and he is going to be missed my many who knew him. John's son is making these lures on a limited basis, but we can't be sure of their continued availability.

> When you see a lot of baitfish, try a popper. Fish it slow and make plenty of splashes.

You should fish needlefish plugs painstakingly slowly. When you think you are going slow enough, you then need to slow down even more. I didn't believe it myself at first when these lures became very popular in the early 1980s, but it's true.

Rigging

Too many anglers simply tie surface lures onto the end of their line and toss them into the sea. End of story. There are, however, many things that you should be doing to increase your chances of landing that big fish if it should hit your lure.

Shock Leaders

When fishing with almost any type of lure, either poppers or swimmers, you should use a long shock leader of 30- to 50-pound-test monofilament or fluorocarbon. First, the shock leader prevents abrasions from cutting through your main line, especially in rocky shallow-water areas. Another consideration is that monster striper bass have large spines, big sharp scales, and gill plates that can easily fray or cut a thinner casting line. If they get any part of your main line alongside their body (and they often do) they will cut through it from rubbing against it in no time. Also, a heavier shock leader won't break when you grab hold of it to land the fish. I attach the shock leader to the main line with a loop-to-loop connection and use double or triple surgeon's loops to form the loops on both the main line and the shock.

Change the rear trebles on your lure to single hooks and dress them with bucktail or feathers.

Many people think that stripers are leader shy, but when I was a boy, my first fishing reel was a Penn Squidder loaded with 36-pound-test Ashway Dacron line. In most cases we would tie our lures directly to that line. Leader material then was called "cat gut" and not readily available, nor affordable for everyone. Not only did we tie directly to what now would qualify as rope, but the line had its own unique smell as well. And guess what? We still caught fish, despite the fact that we were using line that was clearly visible to even a blind fish and stunk, to boot. The point is that it didn't make any difference then nor does it make all that much difference today.

There may be situations and specific areas where going to a lighter-test leader will catch you more fish. But one time that it won't matter much is in the spring, when hungry striped bass have just migrated up the coast, and the only thing on their minds is eating.

I once fished with a guy who always fished with a wire leader while he was surfcasting live eels. Like everyone else, I thought he was crazy. That was one of the cardinal rules you didn't break: Don't use wire when trying to catch a striper. Over a ten-year period he caught as many if not more fish than most other guys, and his fish were also big.

No Snap Swivel

Most guys like using a Cross-Loc or Duo-Loc snap swivel. There are two problems to be aware of. First, Cross-Loc snaps often don't fit inside the eye on the front of the lure, as many lures have the eye set too far back inside the head. Second, the Cross-Loc's end loop is too small for the lure to swing properly. Duo-Loc snaps are easy to use and allow you to change lures quickly, but they can easily open when a big fish gets the right leverage against the lure and the snap. I've lost many fish to this flaw over the years.

When you notice a big fish follow your surface popper or swimmer back to the boat and then refuse to take it, come back with a sinking bait or smaller lure—many times, they'll hit it.

When you tie directly to your leader, you cut down on the possibility of tackle failure. If that piece of gear doesn't exist, it can't fail. Tie your lure on with a good loop knot, such as Lefty's nonslip loop, and it will not only work better, you'll have a much stronger connection to your lure, as well as to the fish. It takes more time, but it's worth the effort.

Adding Bucktail or Feathers

I make sure that almost all of my big swimmers and poppers have single hooks that are dressed with bucktail. Rapalas and Zara Spooks are so finely tuned that removing hooks and adding bucktail or feathers ruins their actions. When I replace the hooks on these lures, I use a small food scale to weigh the hooks and try to match a single hook's weight to the exact weight of the treble I've removed. If you do choose to put bucktail or feathers on these two, make sure you tie them sparsely.

Bucktails are good teasers when used on the back of lures and swimmers. Tie them in various colors and sizes, depending on the predominant size of the baitfish.

Droppers

When the fishing gets tough during the summer and early fall, experienced anglers like to use a dropper rig, which is usually a fly of some sort tied on a dropper loop or tied to the bottom of the leader's swivel approximately 18 to 20 inches in front of a large swimming lure.

Some believe that you only catch smaller bass with this rig, which is true to some degree. However, Tony Stetzko, of Cape Cod, caught a world-record striped bass from shore using this technique. Interestingly enough, that huge fish (some 73 pounds) ate his dropper fly and not the big swimmer.

Droppers can be flies of any size, soft plastics such as Slug-Gos or Fin-S Fish, strips of pork rind, and many other things. Just use your imagination. When fished in the early pre-dawn hours or right after sunset, it can and does account for some nice fish. One of the best spots to fish this rig is where tidal rivers and creeks dump into deeper water. The currents there make the dropper swim as you reel it in.

Flies

If you want to catch a big striper on a fly, you generally need to fish large flies, unless the fish are keying on smaller baits. I have simplified my fly selection over the years (like I have my lure selection) from carrying hundreds of patterns to less than a dozen in a selection of sizes and colors like white, black, yellow, chartreuse, blue and white, and green and white to cover most water conditions. I do not constantly change my flies, preferring to focus on location and presentation first. Too many fly anglers take too much time changing flies for almost no sane reason. All that time spent changing a fly can be better spent with your line in the water fishing one of these patterns correctly and in the right areas.

In the spring I like a 7- to 10-inch-long White Ghost Herring (see photo and recipe on page 187). As the season progresses, and squid patterns become effective, I use a 6- to 7-inch-long White Ghost Squid Fly (see photo and recipe on page 186). This pattern worked so well on our film shoot with Lefty for Bass Pro Shops that he asked me to tie

In addition to showing the fish two flies, dropper rigs also imitate a large fish chasing a smaller one. Attach your lure, usually a swimmer, to a section of 18- to 20-inch 50-pound monofilament. Attach a swivel to the other end of the mono. Tie a short piece of mono to the lower eye of the swivel and attach a fly or other lure.

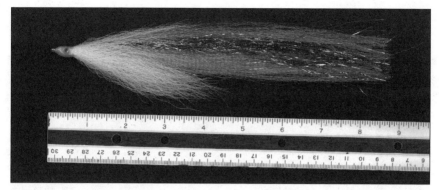

Lefty's Magnum Deceiver is one of the best big-fish flies out there today. Testimony to its effectiveness is how many times it has been copied. *Lefty Kreh photo*

some for him. One of them now hangs in his office where he ties his flies. When fish start feeding on adult menhaden, I use a large White Ghost Menhaden, tied about a foot long or more. These giant flies are best tied with some type of synthetic fiber. Not only is long bucktail hard to come by, but the synthetic sheds water a lot easier and you get more bulk without the weight.

WHITE GHOST MENHADEN

Hook:	#4/0-#5/0 Matzuo O'Shaughnessy
Rattle:	Crystal E-Z Body over a glass rattle, and coated with epoxy
Underbody:	Sparse bucktail 3 to 4 inches long, tied below the shank
Overbody:	White, yellow, and pink yak hair mixed with yellow and rainbow Krystal Flash. Top with black yak hair.
Head:	Black thread
Eyes:	Large red and black doll's eyes coated with epoxy
Note:	The fly should be approximately 8 to 12 inches long

Other flies that I carry are Lefty's Magnum Deceiver and Grocery Fly, which is a Deceiver with lead wire on the hook shank. These large flies are good when there are menhaden and herring in the area.

White Ghost Menhaden with rattle inside the body. This pattern works extremely well when bass are feeding on menhaden. For recipe, see page 111.

Clouser and Kreh's big Half and Half works well all the time, and I usually choose one when fishing near or around some type of structure. It gets a bit deeper, the hook rides up so it doesn't easily get fouled, and the jigging motion can trigger fish into eating it as it passes by. Popovics' fly patterns also work very well. I fish his Bucktail Deceiver and Siliclone to imitate herring or menhaden and the Shady Lady Squid in the spring during the squid runs. All these patterns should be as long as you can get them—as least 6 to 10 inches.

> Tie your lures directly to your leader without any snaps, using a loop knot.

For surface fishing I tie big deer-hair flies spun from coarse deer hair and give them long hackle-feather tails with just a slight amount of flash. I find that putting too much flash in the fly attracts more bluefish. You can also make eel flies from spun deer hair, which are effective when the water is calm very early in the morning or late in the evening just after dark.

Clouser and Kreh's Half and Half accounts for a lot of our big fish through a season. These heavier flies can get down quickly and stay there and can be tied to represent baitfish, big lobsters, and more.

A spun deer-hair fly sits on the surface and leaves a distinctive V wake that attracts big fish when the water is calm. It's an excellent shallow-water fly.

Rattles

I know that many anglers and experts say rattles make little or no difference, but I have to disagree. At many times and in many situations, adding rattles to my lure or fly has made all the difference. When the water is dirty, silted, roiled, or muddy, as it can be in a river after a storm or a lot of runoff, rattles can be a big advantage. Also, when you fish a bit deeper or in low light—during the night or just before sunrise or sunset—a rattle is a distinct advantage in helping a big fish locate a lure or fly that it otherwise might ignore. Also, lures with rattles can be especially effective in rocky areas, as this is the habitat of crabs and lobsters, and the rattles may imitate the snapping of their claws.

Fish any new lure during the day so you can see exactly how it works.

CHAPTER 8

SOFT PLASTICS

Sometimes when fishing with hard lures such as plastic or wood, you have only a split second to set the hook before the fish detects a fraud. With plastic lures you get an extra second or two before they realize it's not the real thing. It's impossible to cover all the soft baits here, as the subject is just too broad. I wrote an entire book on soft plastics called *How to Fish Plastic Baits in Saltwater*. I will, however, look at a few lures that have continually produced big fish for me and my clients over the years.

Fin-S Fish

The 7½-inch and the 10-inch Fin-S Fish are among the most overlooked soft-plastic baits on the market. Although they are popular in some areas, especially in river systems and freshwater impoundments around the country, it's surprising that they haven't gained wider acceptance among saltwater anglers.

The Fin-S Fish is a wide-bodied bait that tapers to a slender, forked tail. Its shape and design allows it to glide, dive, swerve, and twitch

Shaw Grigsby displays the Double Zulu shad rig he invented on the spot when we filmed together. It accounted for well over 200 fish over the next two and a half days of fishing.

when fished properly. This erratic action drives fish wild, and they usually annihilate the bait when they strike. Fin-S Fish can be fished throughout the water column. White, black, and Arkansas Shiner have accounted for many big striped bass on my boat.

Modifications

The Fin-S Fish comes with a #9/0 worm-style hook, which acts as a keel to stabilize the lure when being retrieved. The hook lies inside the belly cavity, and its point sticks out the top. After many years of using these baits, I have arrived at a different system. I toss the packaged hook away. It's hard to sharpen, too thick in diameter, and its position inside the bait causes an awful lot of missed strikes. Instead, I use a #7/0 or #9/0 Matzuo sickle hook, which has a unique bend in its shank that lets it stick out and away from the bait's body for a better hook-set.

Capt. Jim White with a nice bass that ate a 10-inch Fin-S Fish. This plastic lure is deadly on big bass. It was the first split-tail bait ever developed and had been used extensively in fresh water for big landlocked stripers.

Before putting the hook inside the bait, I wrap the shank from the eye to the bend with EE rod-winding thread and apply a few drops of a waterproof glue such as Zap-A-Gap to keep the hook in place and prevent the bait from tearing after repeated casts. Insert the hook's point in the head, push it down and out through the body cavity, and you're ready to fish. I also will add stick-on eyes.

The 7½-inch model is effective on the surface and below. When used with a jighead, cut a small piece off the head of the bait so it fits flush against the head of the jig. The water will flow over the head and the bait better, preventing the bait from rolling over as you retrieve it.

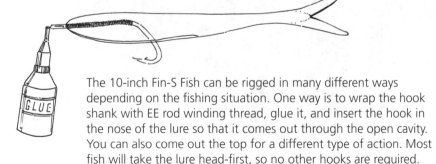

The 10-inch Fin-S Fish can be rigged in many different ways depending on the fishing situation. One way is to wrap the hook shank with EE rod winding thread, glue it, and insert the hook in the nose of the lure so that it comes out through the open cavity. You can also come out the top for a different type of action. Most fish will take the lure head-first, so no other hooks are required.

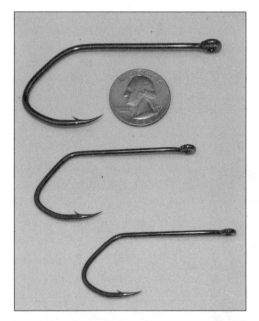

The Matzuo Sickle hook is great for rigging plastics and using as a chassis for flies. They are strong, sharp, and inexpensive. Their black chrome finish is resistant to rust, and I've only had a handful break on me over the years.

Glue, bobbin, thread, and wrapped hooks for rigging soft plastics.

Slug-Gos

This bait is probably one of the deadliest artificials ever invented. Its long, slender profile allows it to dart and dive like a real injured bait-fish. The Slug-Go and the Fin-S Fish are both products of Lunker City Fishing Specialists, which is owned by Herb Reed, the baits' inventor. Each of these baits was the first of its kind, and everything else since then has been a copy.

The 7½-inch Slug-Go can also be used for big fish in the same manner and rigged the same way as the bigger baits. The smaller size is good for a more subtle presentation on a calm day when you want your bait to enter the water quietly or when the predominant bait is relatively small.

When fishing the larger plastic baits, such as the 9-inch Slug-Go and the 10-inch Fin-S Fish, it's best to use a heavy-action

> Thread plastic beads on your line ahead of your plastic lures when the water is roiled or muddy. They will click, and help fish find your bait.

spinning or bait-casting rod for their hook-setting power. Big fish have bony jaws, and the farther away from you that a fish strikes, the more power you'll need to get a good hook-set.

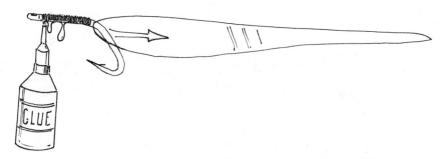

Insert the tip of the hook inside the head of the Slug-Go just before gluing it. Place a small amount of cyanoacrylate glue on the wrappings and push the hook shank inside the body of the bait.

A beautiful keeper-size striper taken on a Slug-Go early in the morning right after sunrise. While fishing live bunker, I like to fish artificials to see what the area holds.

Rigging

The 9-inch Slug-Go also comes packaged with a #9/0 worm hook, which I replace with either a #7/0 or #9/0 Mustad O'Shaughnessy, a #8/0 Matzuo, or a #6/0 Gamakatsu bait hook. Most of the time I use only a single hook in the head, with the point exposed. This increases the hook-up ratio immensely.

By placing the hook's point either facing down on the round side or up on the flat side, you can change how the bait rides in the water. If the point comes out of the bottom, the bait will ride higher, as the flat surface on top causes the bait to plane toward the surface. If the point comes out the top, the bait dives deeper.

Sometimes it pays to rig the 9-inch Slug-Go with two hooks—one in the head and one in the tail. This works well when the fish aren't hitting aggressively. The #6/0 Gamakatsu bait hook is good for this type of rigging. To rig double hooks, you'll need a rigging needle and some 50-pound-test Dacron line.

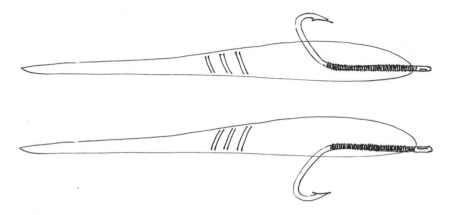

Slug-Gos can be rigged similarly to Fin-S Fish, with single or double hooks that come out the top or bottom. By coming out the bottom, the lure will ride deeper, and by coming out the top the lure will plane and ride higher in the water.

This 12-inch double-rigged Slug-Go is an excellent replica of a live eel and has accounted for many big stripers in recent years.

You can also rig the Slug-Go in reverse. By placing a hook in the tail end, the Slug-Go will fish like a Pencil Popper on the surface. Use a #3/0 O'Shaughnessy hook, as the tail section is thin and you don't want to rip the plastic. Wrap the shank with EE rod-winding thread, and glue it in place when you are finished. Leave about an inch and a half from the tail to the hook eye. Glue two big doll eyes or a pair of 3-D stick-on eyes toward the rear of the body for an excellent squid imitation. A squid-colored Slug-Go is available for an even more realistic presentation. When you fish the bait rigged this way, it will splash, pop, and create a trail of bubbles along the surface as you work it back toward you.

There are at least twelve different ways to rig and fish Slug-Gos. They can be rigged as poppers; rigged on jigheads; fished in tandem, either glued together, arranged one ahead of the other, or combined with a Fin-S Fish; fished deep on a three-way rig; and a host of other ways. If you use your imagination, the Slug-Go is one of the most versatile baits ever invented.

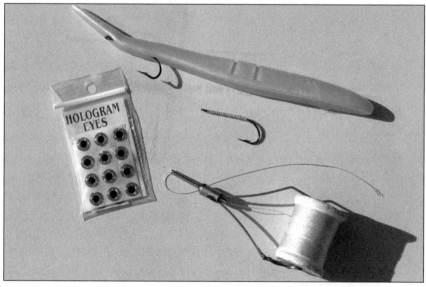

A Slug-Go rigged in reverse will ride high like a Zara Spook and dance from side to side. The thin, flexible tail will whip back and forth, leaving a trail of bubbles on the surface. Use a smaller #2/0 or #3/0 hook for the tail so that it doesn't tear and wrap it with thread so you can glue it in place. Glue a big doll eye on the fat end for a great squid imitation.

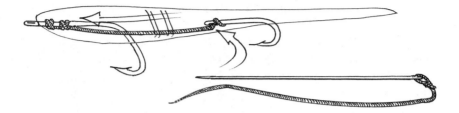

You can also rig a Slug-Go like a dead eel. 1. Double a length of 50- or 60-pound-test Dacron line, tie a knot at the top, and thread the loop end through the hook eye. 2. Thread the rigging needle through the body of the Slug-Go, beginning about three inches up from the tail, and push the needle through the body as close to center as possible, exiting the center of the head at the top. 3. Place the knotted end over the hook on the rigging needle, pull it through all the way, and position the tail hook in the rear of the body. 4. Move the top hook so the point just sticks out of the body. With the rest of the line, tie a series of half-hitches up the shank to the hook eye and tie off with two or three overhand knots. 5. Insert the hook point into the head of the lure, usually down far enough so the barb is inside the head. Before moving the entire hook into the body of the lure, place a few drops of waterproof cyanoacrylate glue on the thread wraps and then move the rest of the hook into position. Once the glue takes hold (usually in a few seconds) the hook will stay in place, even after you have caught a few fish.

Ronz Lures

The Ronz is a long, thin, oval bait that has been soaked in menhaden oil, giving it a natural scent. The baits range in size from 6 inches to over 14 inches. The largest are used to catch school tuna.

The key feature of the Ronz is a smaller and lighter jighead that sinks faster and farther than a conventional one, which is almost two and a half times its size and weight. This allows you to fish

Small Slug-Gos are great worm imitations, and you can fish them on fly rods.

a bigger piece of plastic much deeper while using a smaller jig. This unique jighead system also gives the bait a lifelike action in the water. You can swim it or jig it, and its body responds in a snake-like motion similar to a live eel. It's especially effective in shallow water, as you can use a small jighead that won't sink quickly to the bottom.

Bass Kandy Delight

At 10 inches long and with a thick shad-type body and long tail, the Bass Kandy Delight (BKD) is one mouthful for a big striper. The first season that I used one, I took five fish over 30 pounds and lost at least twice that many. The bait has its own unique action that big stripers just seem to love.

They can be rigged like a Slug-Go or any similar plastic bait. A single hook, placed in the head, is usually sufficient for most conditions. However, BKDs can be rigged with a double hook, placed on a jighead, or even trolled with a special swim-plate head available on some models. The plastic it's made from is extremely tough.

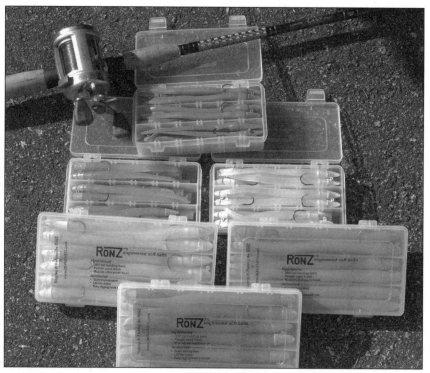

Ronz lures account for some pretty impressive catches. Their special jigheads coupled with the added menhaden scent draw big fish to them like ants to a picnic.

Squid Lures

Squid are one of the baits most sought-after by almost all species of gamefish. They are available worldwide both inshore and offshore. Along the Eastern seaboard, they range from Maine to Florida. They migrate to inshore coastal waters in the spring and fall. The spring run usually sees the large adults at the mouths of bays, and during the fall, the run includes more young-of-the-year, with lengths ranging from 2 to 4 inches. Long used in the offshore fishery for tuna, sharks, marlin, and other pelagic species, squid baits never really caught on with the inshore crowd.

Some brands of plastic squid are as close to true-to-life as you can get. Normally, I'd say that exact duplicates of bait aren't worth that much—the Slug-Go and Fin-S Fish don't really copy anything swimming in the ocean, yet they are deadly when fished correctly. Squid are

Plastic squid imitations are excellent lures when the squid are running in the spring. They can be rigged with or without a weight and fished in shallow water to attract nice bass like this one.

A Lindy Tiger Tube (bottom) and a pink 10-inch Fin-S Fish are good replicas of live squid.

the one exception to the rule, since the fish are so used to seeing and eating them. Plastic squid also come in luminescent colors.

If there is one squid style that's different from all the rest, it would be the Tiger Tube from Lindy Tackle Company out of Brainerd, Minnesota. At 8 inches long and with a round body, hollow interior, and long legs, it looks more like a giant freshwater tube bait than a squid. This lure can be fished on the surface, just below the surface, or off the bottom if weighted. It is extremely effective in fooling big shallow-water stripers.

You can rig and fish the many other squid baits available in a variety of methods. Tsunami, the Berkley Gulp line, and a host of other brands will work. To some of the smaller squids I attach a swim plate and fish the bait close to the surface. I remove the bait from a Berkley Dancing swimbait and replace it with a 4- or 5-inch squid body. The squid's wobbling action close to the surface drives fish wild.

Rigging

The Tiger Tube's hollow body cavity lends itself to many different rigging options and variations of presentation under a wide variety of conditions. By filling the cavity with foam, cork, or some other buoyant material, you can make the bait float on the surface. You can also stuff the cavity with scented cotton balls to leave a natural scent trail while you fish it or add weights or a jig head for a deeper presentation in water up to eight or ten feet.

Our clients have taken stripers up to 42 pounds on floating Tiger Tubes dragged over shallow-water rock fields in water less than 5 feet deep. When a striper takes one of these squid imitations off the surface, the explosion is awesome and the force of the strike arm-wrenching. For this type of fishing, rig the bait with an #8/0 or #9/0 Matzuo sickle hook or an Owner #11/0 worm hook. Before filling the body cavity with foam, position the hook inside so the foam holds it in place as it sets and hardens. We use ordinary insulation foam in a can, available at hardware stores.

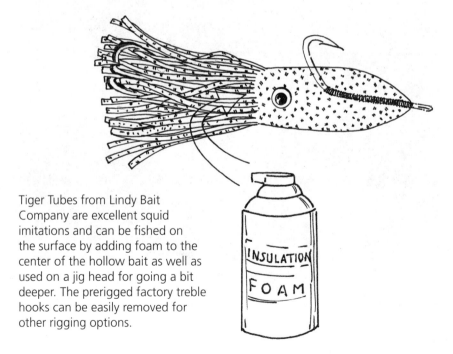

Tiger Tubes from Lindy Bait Company are excellent squid imitations and can be fished on the surface by adding foam to the center of the hollow bait as well as used on a jig head for going a bit deeper. The prerigged factory treble hooks can be easily removed for other rigging options.

Gear and Technique

Tiger Tubes can be fished with heavier tackle when targeting big stripers. I use a Quantum Iron IR4X bait-casting reel with a 7-foot Quantum Affinity swimbait rod and 20-pound test Sufix or Ande monofilament. This beefy outfit can handle big fish, but it's light enough to cast all night without blowing out your arms or shoulders.

Use small swimbaits to search the water for active fish—they can be cast and worked quickly to cover a lot of water fast. Once you find fish, slow down and use larger baits to target the bigger fish.

After you cast the bait, work it in a series of quick, one-two-three-stop motions, and then add an occasional long sweep of the rod to pull the bait across the surface. What you are trying to do is mimic the flight of a scared squid that is being pursued by a big predator and trying to avoid being eaten.

Soft-plastic shad bodies fished on jigheads are excellent big-fish baits. Also known as swim shads or swimbaits, they are easy to use due to their built-in tail-swimming action. *Joe Manansala photo*

Swimbaits

The swimbait craze actually began in fresh water some years ago. Mister Twister is credited with developing the first plastic shad-body swimbait for freshwater anglers back in the 1980s. From there, the field has evolved to include realistic baits that are 8 to 15 inches long. In fresh water, swimbaits of 6 or 8 ounces are common and are responsible for winning thousands of dollars in tournaments throughout the country. The trend has even spawned specialized rods to handle these huge pieces of plastic, which provides saltwater anglers with an additional tool for brine, especially for striped bass. With a resurgence of adult menhaden along our coast, these big-bait imitations have accounted for some impressive catches in recent years.

Swimbaits (sometimes called shad bodies) have been referred to as "the mindless bait," because you can catch fish by just casting them out and reeling them in. There is, however, a bit more to it than that

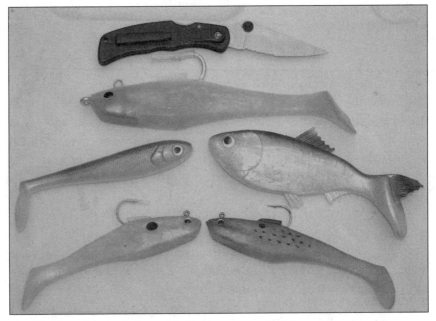

Shad bodies of various sizes and shapes are easy to fish and they lure big stripers. You can fish them deeply by adding jigheads.

Shad bodies, such as these from Tsunami, Storm, and Panther Martin, can be fished in shallow water, near the surface, or down deep if necessary. They have a wide range of uses and should be part of every angler's kit.

to be really successful. Most swimbaits come with a weight already built into their bodies. Others can be rigged with various size jig-heads and different head shapes. When fishing in shallow water, you want a swimbait that is not too heavy and has the ability to suspend or sink slowly to the bottom, factors influenced by weight and re-trieve speed. As long as the bait remains upright and swims correctly, it will catch fish.

You can control actions with the rod tip and line retrieve. Stop and go, lift and drop, speed up forward, sweep and rip fast, and other meth-ods will greatly increase the bait's effectiveness. These baits can also be fished and rigged sideways so the body is actually fished flat on its side for a totally new action and presentation. Stick with the basic colors that you would likely select for any artificial bait—white, yellow, char-treuse, and black—and then add colors such as bunker, mackerel, or herring when these baitfish are present.

Soft Plastics for Fly Rods

Fly rods in the 10- and 11-weight range are capable of handling many of the soft plastics on the market today, especially 3- to 6-inch Slug-Gos and 3- to 4-inch Fin-S Fish. If you glue the baits to the hook shank, they will stay in place, even when you cast them. These baits can be especially effective during the Northeast's fabled worm hatches. Plastics in red and bubblegum are excellent during the worm swarm. When worms are hatching, they tend to draw big fish as well as the smaller fish. Most fish are going to be small during this time, but anglers have caught many big fish as well. If you are willing to experiment and try new techniques, then this is one that is worth the time. Many times, the 2- and 3-inch Slug-Gos will work better than almost any type of fly, and, in my opinion, the object of this game is to catch fish.

A Storm swim shad fooled this nice striper. Swim shads are effective lures for big stripers, and they are easy to use, even for inexperienced anglers. Since the action is already built in, you simply cast one out, reel it in, and the bait does most of the work for you.

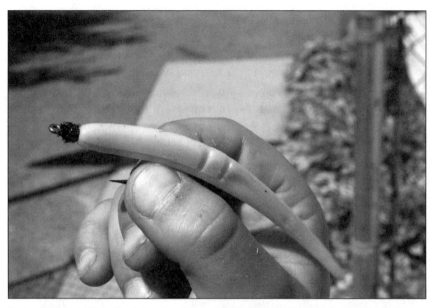

A single 3-inch Pink Slug-Go that has a head wrapped with peacock herl to help imitate a small sand worm. This lure works better than most worm flies.

For the 2- and 3-inch Slug-Gos, I use a #1 Matzuo O'Shaughnessy hook. Wrap the hook shank with thread and then glue the bait onto the hook to keep it in place when you cast. If you use a 9- or 10-weight rod, you can fish two or three at a time. They are easy to cast with a floating line and an 8- or 9-foot leader. Retrieve them in short quick strips so they dart and dive like they are supposed to. The fish will take care of the rest.

For colors I like bubblegum, red shad, black, and green watermelon. All look like sea worms that are spawning. To make them even more effective, you can add a peacock herl head to imitate the natural.

CHAPTER 9

LIVE BAIT

MORE BIG STRIPED BASS have fallen for live bait than almost all other methods combined. The reason is simple: It's what bass eat on a daily basis. And when they do eat, they want a meal that will fill them up quickly. Using live bait effectively and properly requires knowledge, skill, and a total understanding of your quarry.

In this chapter I concentrate on the five main types of bait readily available to most anglers no matter where you live or fish. There are probably a few localized exceptions due to a bait's natural range, but if you fish anywhere from Maine to the Carolinas, at least one or more of them will be within your reach. Many other types of bait will work as well as the ones listed below. Many anglers like using mackerel, live scup (porgies), crabs, mullet, sand eels, and no doubt countless others. Again, a lot depends on where you are fishing at the time, as each section of the coast has its own preferences.

Menhaden

These oily, smelly baitfish are also known as pogies, bunker, moss-bunker, and by other local names as well. Menhaden roam the Eastern seaboard in vast schools and move to inshore bays, rivers, and coves during the late spring and early summer. Menhaden are one of the most sought-after baitfish along the Atlantic seaboard and considered one of the most important baitfish in the sea. They are eaten by virtually every large predator swimming around out there.

Menhaden are also highly sought by commercial fishermen, who use boats as well as planes to spot the huge schools and then net them by the thousands. Unfortunately, humans as well as gamefish want menhaden for their oil, which is used in making soap, cosmetics, pet food, and more. The Omega III protein found in their oil is considered valuable in preventing heart disease. All this attention has driven the numbers of menhaden to very low levels in many areas of their normal range and has triggered controversy between recreational and com-

Dawn is just breaking as this angler gets his bait for the day before the sun gets too high in the sky.

A live menhaden hooked through the nose cavity with a #3/0 VMC treble hook. Live pogies are excellent big-striper baits.

mercial anglers on how many should be taken from any given bay or cove during the season. Legislation is currently pending in Congress to protect the Atlantic menhaden from further depletion, as lawmakers become more educated and aware of just how valuable this baitfish is to the environment, including the gamefish that feed upon them.

In terms of the best bait for monster striped bass, I'd have to say that the menhaden is tops, even better than live eels. I know there are probably many who will disagree with that statement. But I have used both for many years and menhaden are the hands-down winner. When the predominant bait is menhaden and they arrive in good numbers, striped bass can't help themselves when feeding on them. As far as a big striper is concerned, a pogie is heroin and cocaine all rolled into one. They are simply that addicted to them. I have gone to an area and fished it hard with almost everything I had in the boat without so much as a bump or even a chase from a striped bass. But toss in a live bunker, and the fish come out of nowhere and from everywhere to eat it. I've seen this so many times that I'm convinced absolutely nothing will outfish a live menhaden.

An angler using a small gill net to get his live menhaden for the day's fishing. This is more efficient than snagging them, and your baits aren't injured or cut up either. However, it always doesn't work, and there are times when snagging is the only way you will get them. *Joe Manansala photo*

Catching Menhaden

The best baits to use are the freshest ones you can get your hands on. Frozen baits will work, but they are not nearly as effective as fresh ones. Menhaden are caught by cast-netting, by using a small gill net, or by the most popular method, snagging.

They need to be in relatively shallow water to toss a cast net over them or they'll swim out from underneath the net as it drops. They also have to be packed together pretty tightly, and even then, throwing a cast net effectively takes a lot of practice.

In some areas, anglers use a small gill net. This may not be legal in some states, so check your local regulations carefully before you go out and buy one. Gill nets are usually set after dark or just before dawn. Their effectiveness diminishes dramatically once the sun comes up.

When you find menhaden in the middle of a bay or river, where

Cast nets of various sizes are used to collect live bait without injuring them. They take some practice, but the effort is worth the reward because snagging is time consuming.

they move quickly, snagging is the best option. You cast a bare hook out into a school and simply yank through it until you snag one. You can buy commercially made snag rigs at many bait shops along the coast. This rig is nothing more than a big treble hook with a molded piece of lead on its shank for weight, so you can cast it and let it sink beneath a school.

A much better way is to tie your own. This is how the pros do it: First, tie a two- or three-ounce sinker on the end of 50-pound-test leader material. Six to eight inches above the sinker, tie a dropper loop onto the leader and attach a #5/0 or #6/0 treble hook with a loop knot. Then tie on another treble hook just above the first in the same manner. At the top of the rig, tie on a swivel to attach to your main line.

This gives you two sets of trebles to snag with at once. What's nice about this rig is that a standard treble hook is usually made of finer gauge wire than the ones in the store-bought rigs. This means the hook point and barb are thinner and they don't tend to rip and tear the flesh of the bait like heavier hooks. Also, with the weight at the bottom of the rig, there is less pressure against the fish as he struggles to free himself. You therefore lose fewer fish, and they won't bleed as badly once they're in the boat.

Cast well beyond any breaking and flipping baitfish, and let your rig sink to the bottom. Retrieve your rig up and through the school, coming from the bottom up to the top. Many times you can actually feel

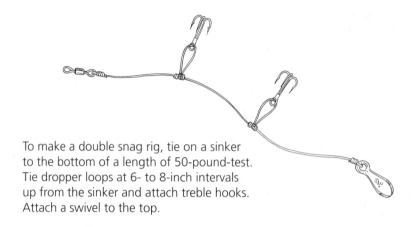

To make a double snag rig, tie on a sinker
to the bottom of a length of 50-pound-test.
Tie dropper loops at 6- to 8-inch intervals
up from the sinker and attach treble hooks.
Attach a swivel to the top.

the pogies bang against your line. In fact, that is one technique used
by commercial rod and reel anglers. When the schools aren't on the
surface, they look for them using electronics. Once a school is located,
they make a cast, let the snag rig sink, and then reel in slowly, waiting
for tell-tale bumps against their line. When they feel a bump, they then
yank the rig upward and usually snag a baitfish.

For snagging, I find a rod that isn't too stiff will get you a lot more
bait a lot quicker than a stiffer rod. Stiff rods tend to rip and tear at the
flesh once the pogie is snagged, thus causing many to escape. Snagging
pogies is work and losing one is aggravation to the nth degree. Each
one lost is time wasted, especially in the morning when you are trying
to make a tide. Fiberglass rods are excellent. I've had two 7-foot fiberglass rods custom-made for this purpose.

Once you have your bait, you need to take care of it. Any baitfish
that is bleeding badly should be placed in a bucket of water until the
flow stops before putting it in the live well. Any excess blood or a
buildup of blood in the live well or bait tank will quickly kill all the
rest of the menhaden inside.

Whatever type of live-well system you have, make sure to constantly change the water to keep oxygen levels high so the bait stays alive
and healthy. In my main live well, which circulates the water automatically, I've also added an aerator stone that pumps oxygen bubbles into
the water to supplement the water-exchange system. This has helped

Here is a simple rig for snagging menhaden. Notice that the lead has already been molded around the hook's shank for added weight. Some anglers like this rig; others prefer the dropper method.

tremendously in keeping more bait alive for longer periods of time. The aerator stone runs off a small, 12-volt motorcycle battery that I installed for this purpose. I have kept a dozen or more baits alive for two or three days using this system, which saves precious time in the morning if bait is hard to come by.

Some boats don't have bait tanks in them and many surf casters certainly don't have bait tanks built into their vehicles. You can make your own bait tank from big buckets or even coolers or purchase premade tanks that are on the market today. All you need is a bilge pump, some hose, and a battery (12-volt) to run the pump. Make sure the tank you select is round or oval in shape as most baitfish swim in circles, especially menhaden. Avoid square corners at all cost.

If you prefer fishing menhaden dead or chunked on the bottom, place them in ice and don't let them lie in melted ice water. For long-term care, brine them in a mixture of kosher salt and water to preserve the slime coating on their skin and toughen it at the same time.

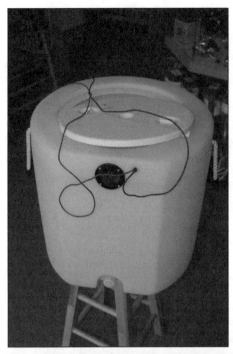

(Left) Small live-bait tanks can be installed in smaller boats or even in a vehicle to allow you to transport fresh live bait almost anywhere. All you need to add to most of these units is a 112-volt battery to run the pump system.

(Below) Fresh menhaden—the fresher the better—make excellent cut bait when fished on the bottom. Many times, stripers will prefer a chunk of bait on the bottom over live bait. Why? Who knows?

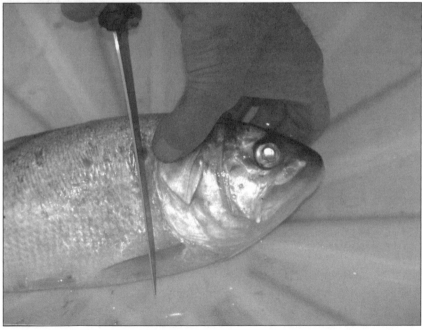

Fishing Menhaden

For live-lining menhaden, hook your bait through the nose cavity located just on the end of the snout, which has a bone above the nostril that will hold your hook in place nicely. Toss them out and let them swim around next to or over structure. The bass will take care of the rest. There are other ways of hooking them, but I find this method to be the best. You can also hook them in the back at the top just behind the head, and in the tail behind the anal fin. If fish are having a hard time catching our baits (menhaden can swim extremely fast when pursued by big stripers) we snip the tail with a pair of scissors. This will slow the bait down and cause it to swim erratically as the fish tries to eat it.

When a fish takes the bait, let it run with it a bit. Allow your line to tighten down until it becomes taut, and then set the hook in one solid sweeping motion. I usually let the fish go until a count of five or six. Some say to go longer; some say not to wait at all. What I don't want to do is let the fish swallow the bait deeply and gut-hook him. If you fish your live bait properly, you won't hook that many fish deeply. In time,

To build a three-way rig, attach the main line from your reel to one eye on a three-way swivel. On the second eye, tie a 5- to 8-foot leader for your lure or bait. On the last eye, attach a 6- to 10-inch section of light test line and a sinker to it. Bounce this rig on the bottom as you drift.

Make a simple hook remover from a 20-inch section of wooden dowel or old broom stick. At the bottom cut a notch with a Dremel tool or saw so it will fit a hook's shank and then smooth out all edges. At the top drill a lanyard hole and wrap the top with heavy cord for a grip.

you develop a feel for what is the right amount of time to let a fish eat the bait. It's not fool-proof, but well over 90 percent of the fish I catch are hooked in the jaw or somewhere inside the mouth, where hook remov-al is easily accomplished.

For deeply hooked fish, all you need is a simple tool to re-move the hook easily. To make one yourself, cut a V-notch in one end of a wooden dowel about 25 inches long. Wrap the other end of the dowel with thin rope or twine to a grip. To

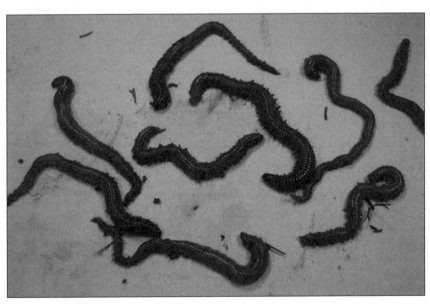

Live sea worms work great on the back of tube-and-worm rigs or can be simply floated beneath a bobber in the current. When drifting them under a bobber, use the biggest worms you can find. When using them on a tube-and-worm rig, smaller ones work well.

Chris Megan of *On the Water* magazine lands a big striper after a bluefish bit off the tail of his live pogy. When that happens, it's a good idea to let the chopped bait sink to the bottom before reeling it in. As Chris shows here, it can pay off.

remove the hook, slide the notch down your line into the fish's mouth, and press the notch against the hook bend. Hold the line tightly against the dowel, and push down and out in one quick motion to dislodge the hook. Nine times out of ten, the fish won't even bleed.

You can also fish menhaden and other baits on a three-way rig in deeper water. A three-way rig is simple to make. First you need a three-way swivel. Tie your line from your reel to one of the eyes. On the second eye you make a 5- to 7-foot leader and attach your hook and bait to it. On the last eye, you use a piece of mono that is lighter than the test of the line you are using and tie a sinker on a piece of 6- to 8-inch-long mono. Drop the rig down to the bottom, and the fish will hopefully take care of the rest. To prevent frequent snags, some like to crank their line up from the bottom three or four turns after the weight hits the bottom, especially when fishing over a rocky bottom. Another way to fish menhaden is to cut them into chunks for bottom fishing. The head and midsections are the best to use for stripers.

Eels

Eels are prized for their ability to lure monster stripers into striking when other baits seem to fail. In Rhode Island, anglers like eels that are so big you can saddle and ride them. In most other areas that I've fished, a much smaller eel is preferred. If I had to pick one size range, it would be 12 to 16 inches. However, two of the biggest stripers I have seen caught were taken on 9- to 10-inch "shoestring eels."

I was taught that eels were only good for night fishing, but that old wives' tale has been disproved many times by countless anglers who have caught big stripers from both shore and boat during the middle of the day while tossing these snakes. They will even work in shallow water when the sun is shining bright. If there is such a thing as a truism in fishing, it is this: Nothing is for certain.

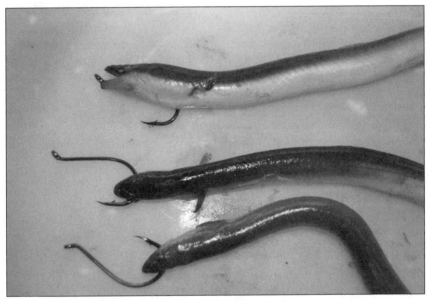

Live eels make excellent bait at night and also during the day when they account for nice catches on flats or cast near rocky shorelines. Three methods of hooking live eels (from top to bottom): Down the throat and out the bottom; between the two eye sockets and bottom; and up through the chin and out the top. The top method is preferred by expert anglers such as Bill "Eel Man" Nolan.

Eels are normally hooked either up through the bottom of the mouth and out the top of the nose or between the two eye sockets. In these methods, the hook rides upright. The third method, which I learned from my good friend Billy "Eel Man" Nolan, is to go down through the mouth, inside the throat, and out through the bottom of the neck, which is completely opposite of the most popular and accepted method of hooking a live eel. Although each method offers its own advantages, you don't argue with someone who earned the nickname "Eel Man." Billy claims that the hook placed in the eel this way acts as a keel and keeps the eel swimming straight.

Billy told me that an old-timer told him about that trick over 25 years ago, and he's used it ever since with great success. The idea is that the eel swims through the water more naturally with its belly down and back facing up as opposed to rolling or turning over on its back when the hook is placed in the upward position. With the hook pointing down, the hook acts as a keel to aid in keeping the eel straight as its reeled in. I now hook all my live eels with the hook facing down instead of up, and the results have been amazing.

One of the best hooks is the Gamakatsu #6/0 Octopus because of its offset shank and angled eye, which makes snelling the hook to the line a breeze. I believe this style of hook gives you a better hook-set when you strike a fish. Use a piece of 18- to 24-inch 50-pound-test mono or fluorocarbon leader. If you use fluorocarbon, make sure you don't spit on it or wet the knot before you pull it tight, as this will only cause it to slip under pressure. I learned this from Lefty Kreh when he was updating his current knot book. At the top, tie on a crane swivel, and you're ready to fish.

Fishing Live Eels

Eels can be fished in a wide variety of ways, but no other method lends itself better to shallow water than the cast-and-retrieve method. Trolling eels slowly at night, in tight to the shoreline, is also effective—but it can be dangerous if you don't know what you're doing. Those who use this method usually do it from an aluminum boat that is capable of banging rocks and reefs with little or no serious damage to the hull.

Cast your eel toward shore or likely looking structure, and retrieve it as

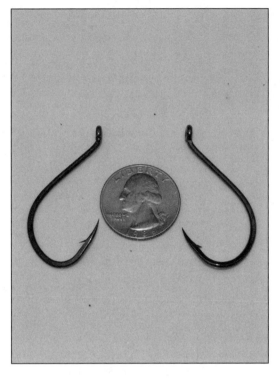

Any #6/0 Octopus-style hook is normally used for fishing live eels. Hooks from Gamakatsu, Eagle Claw, Mustad, and Matzuo all work well. Their bent eye allows you to snell the hook so the leader comes off the hook at a straight angle and gives a better hook-set when a fish takes the eel.

slowly as possible. Casting reels are best suited for eeling because their gear ratio is lower than most of today's spinning reels, which have a high rate of retrieve. The old Penn Z-Series was popular for decades for fishing live eels because its gear ratio was a mere 4:1. A low-ratio line-retrieval system isn't easy to find in today's spinning reels, with the exception of the Van Staal, which is expensive.

Hold your rod even with the water or just slightly elevated as you reel in. When a striper hits an eel, you will feel a distinct bump or bang. You then lower your rod tip toward the fish, let your line tighten, and then strike in a swift, upward motion. There is really no need to let the fish run, as many claim. When you feel that bump, he already has the eel in his mouth. Sometimes the strike is so violent that there isn't any time to give line. The fish almost hooks itself, but you need to be ready for this as it's also a lot easier to lose one when this happens.

Keeping Eels

Eels are best kept alive and on ice, which slows them down and makes them easier to handle. Make sure that the water drains away in the bot-

Eels will catch fish night and day. Choose eels that are 12 to 16 inches in length and use tackle strong enough to get a good hook-set. Medium-heavy to heavy-action rods are best. Any of the freshwater muskie rods are great for fishing live eels.

tom or the eels will drown from their own slime and the water mixing together. Most experienced eel fishermen use a two-bucket system, with one inside of the other, and holes drilled in the bottom of the inside bucket so it drains out into the bottom bucket. Place the ice on top. Grab them with a towel or rag to hook them.

Rigging Dead Eels

Dead eels can be rigged in two ways. First, you can rig them the same way as describe in the chapter on rigging 9- and 12-inch Slug-Gos with a double-hook rig (see page 123). Before hooking the fish, you should break the cartilage in the eel's back so it swims naturally once it's rigged. Pick the eel up with a rag, and, starting at one end, break the cartilage in its back.

You can also attach whole, dead eels to swim plates. As with the double-hook rig, you need to break the eel's back first so that it swims

Swim plates can be rigged with dead eels (most common) or just an eel skin. Place the eel on the swim plate and position the hook so it comes out of the top side of the eel as it lies with the belly facing down. Lash the head to the plate with Dacron line and tie it off at the eye of the swim plate, which is usually molded for this purpose.

naturally. Next, place the hook from the swim plate in the eel's head, usually right behind the eyes. Come up from the bottom beneath the neck so the eel is lying on the plate face-up, in a natural position. Then, secure the head to the plate with Dacron line. Some fishermen like to tie off the ends on the front eye of the plate.

The freshest bait is the best. Make sure your live well is capable of providing enough oxygen to keep your bait lively and fresh.

Smaller eels, ones not bigger than 9 to 12 inches, are best for rigging like this. If the eel is too big, it tends to overwhelm the swim plate and won't swim correctly when you cast it. One of my friends caught a 52-pound striper back in 1986 on an eel rig like this, and the eel was only 9 inches long. It always doesn't take a big snake of two feet or more to catch a big fish.

Rigging Eel Skins

When I was ten or twelve years old, I'd watch my father and uncles skin and rig eels almost every Thursday night so they had enough for the weekend at Cape Cod or in the surf at Newport, Rhode Island. Someone, somewhere, and at sometime figured out that rigging eel skins was just as effective as using the live ones, especially when surf casting or trolling from a boat. I always wanted to meet that guy—he must have been a creative genius.

Fishing with eel skins on plugs and bobs used to be a popular method of fishing back in the 1950s, 1960s, and 1970s. Today however, it's almost a lost art practiced by those who were taught by someone older. It's also a lot of work to rig and skin eels—and it is messy and smelly. At one time bait-and-tackle stores sold fresh eel skins for rigging, but these places are now scarce. Fortunately, I have about six or seven dozen salted away and frozen.

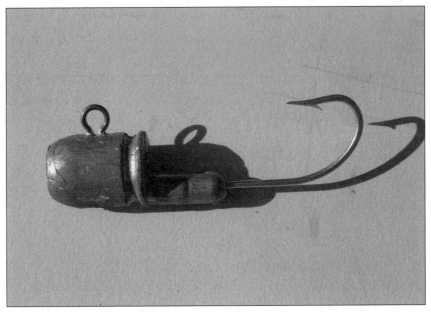

The eel bob was originally developed for fishing strong, heavy currents of the Cape Cod Canal. It's simply a jighead with one or two hooks molded into the body.

The head of the eel bob is hollow to allow water to pass through it. When it's cast into the water, the water flows through the opening in the head and inflates the attached skin, giving the impression of a live eel.

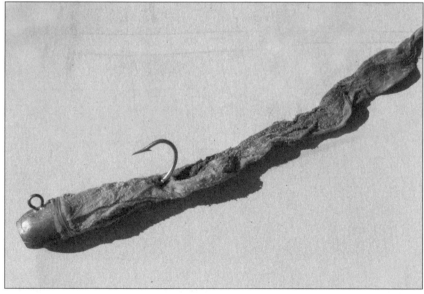

A rigged eel skin on an eel bob. The neck has a collar for securing the eel skin.

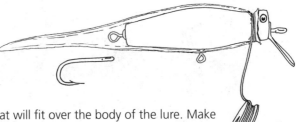

To make an eel-skin plug, remove all the hooks from an old wood swimmer. Use a Dremel to carve out a slot up near the head so you can secure the skin. Select a skin that will fit over the body of the lure. Make sure it doesn't hang over more than two or three inches or the skin will tangle on the tail hook. Once the skin is in place, cut a small hole in the skin at the tail end where the tail hook should be and attach a stainless-steel hook. Keep the lure in a plastic bag with some kosher salt to preserve the skin, and it will last for years.

To skin an eel, first nail its head to a board or fence post. With a very sharp knife or razor blade, cut a circle around the skin in back of the gills. Once you have cut the skin away from the body, grab the loose skin with a pair of pliers and pull down on the skin. This will turn the skin inside out as it comes off of the eel's body.

Place the skins inside a combination of kosher salt and water to preserve them. After they have soaked overnight, place them in a plastic airtight container with more salt, and put them in the freezer to preserve them. I have some that are ten years old. When I thaw them out, they are as good as new.

To rig a swimmer with an eel skin, first remove all the hooks from an old, beat-up swimmer. Cut or file a notch in the head of the lure so you can tie the skin down tightly. Wooden lures are best for this, as they are easier to work with. Next, drape the skin over the lure, starting at the rear and pulling the skin forward so it goes over the cut you've just made. Lash the skin down over the cut with some heavy Dacron line. The tail shouldn't hang over the end of the lure by more than 2 or 3 inches. Any longer and it will continually foul on the rear hook when casting it. Next, cut a small hole at the rear of the plug in the skin right where the rear eyelet is for the tail hook. I attach a single stainless-steel Siwash hook to the rear of the swimmer in size #5/0 to #8/0 depending on the size of the lure I am using. Squeeze the hook's open eye closed with a pair of pliers. The stainless-steel hook prevents rusting from the salt on the skin.

An old wood plug ready to be rigged with an eel skin.

Old-timers would rub the skins with steel wool, sand, a piece of glass, or Brillo pads to make the skins a shiny, bluish color. Many others fished them the way they were. When not in use or when you are done fishing, wrap them in waxed paper, then some newspaper, and put them back in the freezer. Take them out an hour or two before you are ready to fish so they thaw before reaching the water. Placing them in a bucket with some water speeds up the thawing process.

After you cast the eel-skin swimmer, reel it in as slowly as possible. The combination of the slow side-to-side movement of the lure, the tail fluttering in the current, and the scent from the skin will attract any hungry stripers. These lures work as well today as they did forty years ago. Making them just takes some extra time and effort.

There is also a jighead called an eel bob. This unique jig was poured with a hole in its head. When the jig enters the water, the water passes through the opening in the head and inflates the eel skin lashed to it. This rig was used a lot in the strong currents of Cape Cod Canal in Massachusetts, where it is said to have been developed. Some say that bobs are only useful for fast or deep currents, but they are also useful for some shallow-water areas, such as flats that drop off into deeper water. Toss the eel bob up onto the flat and then let it drop off. The weight of the jighead kicks up sand, which alerts any bass to something moving along the bottom. Sometimes the eel is eaten before it gets to the drop-off.

Squid

Squid normally migrate inshore in the spring. This migration can be heavy or hardly noticeable, but bass will almost always follow a good run. Fresh squid is by far the best and will catch you the most and the biggest fish. In most areas, the fresher the squid is, the better, and local squid works better than a lot of store-bought squid that comes from the West Coast, which might not be the same size as the local stock. Use frozen squid only if fresh ones aren't available. Fresh squid can be caught from bridges, piers, causeways, or anywhere lights shine on the water and cast a shadow. Squid fishermen hang special lights over the sides of bridges to attract squid.

Squid can also be caught with squid jigs, which are contraptions that have a series of barbs that point upward in row after row. When a squid grabs hold with its tentacles, it can't free itself. Squid rigs can be fished singularly or in a series of lures on the line attached to dropper loops on the leader. A lead weight is normally attached to the bottom of

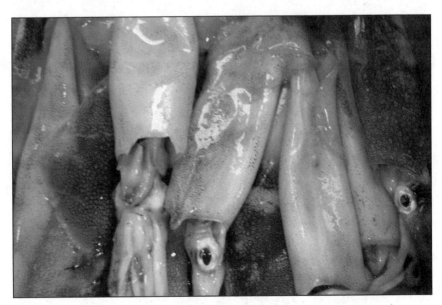

Local, fresh squid is the best bait in the spring when squid are inshore. If you find an area where there are lights on the water, such as from a bridge, you can catch your own, which is an art in itself.

ALEWIVES (RIVER HERRING)

Alewives, or river herring, return to their natal rivers every spring to spawn, and this migration occurs like clockwork. Alewives will normally arrive in spawning rivers in mid to late March, depending on the weather, and then migrate back out to sea in late May or early June. Just like salmon, they will ascend a river system and try to conquer any obstacles put before them. One type of obstacle they can't conquer is a man-made dam. Dams have caused the loss of prime spawning habitat in many of their historic runs, but recently many states have been making efforts to remove dams or install fish ladders so that the alewives can spawn.

In many areas of New England, the alewife was once the most important baitfish in the spring, and anglers would net them at night. During the early part of the season, there is no better live bait than alewives for catching big stripers. Now, due to overfishing and loss of primary habitat, their numbers have been reduced significantly. At one time they literally filled streams and rivers as they ascended toward the freshwater ponds at the headwaters before returning to the sea.

When herring fishing was legal, nice fish like this one could be caught in the spring. Hopefully, herring stocks will rebound, and we'll once again

be able to fish with them. In the meantime, big herring flies or large plugs also work.

Today, a new problem has arisen. The use of pair trawls, used in the offshore sea-herring fishery, which is a totally different species of baitfish, has depleted alewife numbers even further.

At sea, the two species move and migrate

together. When commercial pair trawlers target sea herring, they also capture alewives in their nets. At the present time, the alewife has come under the protection of three New England states—Rhode Island, Massachusetts, and Connecticut—to help restore a once abundant and healthy fishery and to hopefully stem the tide of any further decline. Restrictions have been enacted in all three states to prohibit their use as bait or even their possession while sport fishing. Because of this, it would behoove anyone wishing to use alewives for bait to first check regulations to see if it is legal to catch and possess this baitfish.

the rig and the rig is then lowered from a bridge or pier into the water and jigged up and down next to the lights shining on the water. The squid are attracted by the lights, see the jigs, and grab hold. You simply reel them up and into your bucket or cooler. There is really no need to set the hook as they impale themselves on all those small barbs extending from the jig.

The best way to fish squid in shallow water is beneath a float, bobber, or balloon. Adjust the float to the water depth you are fishing, but keep the squid high enough off the bottom so that it's out of reach of resident bait stealers. Everything that swims likes to eat squid.

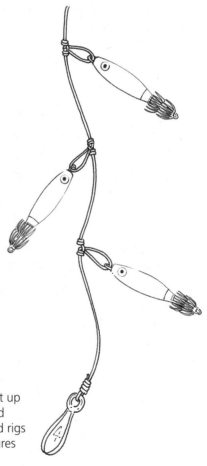

Squid jigs have a series of barbs that point up in row after row. When a squid grabs hold with his tentacles, it can't free itself. Squid rigs can be fished singularly or in a series of lures attached to dropper loops.

Bait with Fly Rods

Many of you may be asking, what if I want to catch a big fish with a fly rod but the fish are totally focused on live bait? Instead of making a whole lot of casts to a good-looking spot and trying different retrieves and flies, which is a lot of work with low-percentage results, you can use the old bait-and-switch method used by offshore anglers for many years. It takes at least two anglers to do effectively. One handles the live bait on one rod, while the second is ready with his fly rod. Coax the fish close to the boat with the bait, take it away from him, and cast a large fly to the excited fish. It's important to make an accurate cast quickly and to immediately strip the fly back close to the live bait in hopes of fooling the fish into eating it instead. A hit from a big striper that's been teased up is arm-wrenching and heart-stopping. You need to be ready for this and to make sure your gear is up to the task, or the fish can quickly break you off.

Hooks for Live Bait

Today, anglers have a wide range of good hooks from which to choose. In fact, unlike years ago when the selection was limited, the number of styles, sizes, and brands can be overwhelming, especially for someone new to the sport.

I only use a few different brands and types of hooks. For live-lining with big river herring, menhaden (pogies), small mackerel, or porgies (also known as scup), I like #2/0 through #4/0 VMC hooks, and I mostly use trebles. For fishing live eels, I like the #6/0 Gamakatsu Octopus. These hooks are very strong and extremely sharp, but also expensive. For most other fishing situations, I like Matzuo hooks from China. They come in a black/chrome finish, are extremely sharp, and, best of all, reasonably priced. Though they can be hard to find, they are worth the effort to ask your favorite tackle shop to order them for you.

Though a lot of people prefer stainless-steel hooks, they have some downsides. First, stainless-steel hooks won't rust out if lost in a fish. Second, stainless-steel hooks tend to be brittle and are easily broken, especially on big fish. There are many hooks on the market today with coatings that last a long time and fight rust.

Matzuo's sickle hook (O'Shaughnessy line) has a bent shank that allows it to sit out and away from rigged bait. This wider bite gives you a better hook-set. I use them for almost all my plastic rigging, and I tie most of my flies on these hooks as well. They resist rust very well and will remain sharp. In over eight years of using these hooks I've had only five bend or break on me, and I go through an awful lot of hooks in a season.

Tackle for Live Bait

In shallow water, you need gear that can survive all types of obstructions and snags, unless you are fishing a structureless beach. Lines should be at least 30- to 40-pound test, with fluorocarbon leaders that test from 60 to 80 pounds. Monster stripers will head for the nearest barnacle-covered rock or ledge or lobster pot that they can find, and you will need lines with good abrasion resistance.

Among the best rods I have used are the muskie or swimbait rods that are now manufactured by many companies, including Quantum and Shimano. They are some of the best rods that you can get without having to get a custom rod, which is very expensive. Tsunami also offers an inexpensive line of rods that are strong, look great, and get the job done. Their new jigging rods and heavy-action bait rods are perfect for this type of fishing.

Reels with a low retrieve ratio are the best for fishing live eels.

I prefer conventional type (casting) reels such as Abu Garcia's 6500 and 7000 series, the Shimano Calcutta and Tekota series, as well as the Quantum Iron IR4X. They have better drags than most spinning reels, and offer a free-spool option as well as a line clicker so you can place the rod in a rod holder while you wait. Some spinning reels offer a baitrunner feature that disengages the spool so the line is free to move, but that line still has to turn over the bail's pick-up arm, and too many things can go wrong. The Shimano Baitrunner spinning reel is considered one of the best on the market today. Okuma has a nice reel as well, and Quantum has introduced its own series of baitrunners for 2009.

CHAPTER 10

SURF FISHING

TO BE HONEST, I don't do an awful lot of surf fishing anymore, as my guide business almost prevents it, and I can't rock hop the way I used to because of a foot injury. With 21 inches of stainless steel in my right foot, it's not a good idea to traverse jagged, barnacle-encrusted rock in total darkness. That being said, I did spend much of my life fishing from the beach as well as from granite outcroppings. As I stated in the introduction, I was fortunate in my youth to have a father and uncles who fished during the golden days of surf fishing and was exposed to some of the best surf casters alive at that time. Hal Woolner, Hal Lyman, Charlie Murat, Jerry Sylvester, Art Lavallee Sr., and others were regulars at the water's edge when I grew up.

What I miss the most about surf fishing is the intimacy of being attached to the beach and the water at the same time. Having the water wash up against your legs and feeling its power and spray while trying to maintain your balance is something everyone who fishes for striped bass should experience. It really does make you feel alive, as well as a part of the striper's environment. Being at the water's edge and watching the sun rise or seeing it set in a golden-red blaze in the evening is something you never forget.

Sunrise or sunset, and not noon, is the best time to be fishing the beach. This angler patiently waits for a bite while fishing a chunk bait on the bottom. *Joe Manansala photo*

On the other hand, I certainly don't miss being knocked down by crashing waves or slipping on grass-covered, oil-soaked rocks in total darkness. I also don't miss the long walks to and from an area where you hope the fish will be, only to find that they're not. When you only have a minimal amount of time to fish to begin with, this can be aggravating.

I also don't buy that fishing in the surf is somehow better or more challenging than fishing from a boat. There is a certain belief among today's surf-fishing crowd that somehow fish caught from a boat don't count as much as those from the beach. Boat fishing has its own set of problems and challenges that go along with doing it effectively and safely. Also, when things go wrong in the surf or conditions worsen as you are fishing, you can simply step back and walk away. In a boat you don't have that option. In my lifetime on the water, I've never seen anyone get out of his boat, walk across the water, and go home for the day because the conditions got bad. Knocking one type of fishing only shows one's ignorance.

Surf Rods

I'm from the old school, so I have old-school thoughts on what's the best type of rod to use for surf casting. I happen to like fiberglass rods, or at least rods that are not totally graphite. Ones made of E-Glass or S-Glass are my favorites. Most of the S-Glass rods are being manufactured by Lamiglas. The E-Glass line has been discontinued by this rod maker. I like the way they feel and handle while casting or fighting a fish. Glass or composite rods allow for longer casts and better fighting qualities than pure graphite rods, which are stiff and not forgiving. The composite rods or rods made of fiberglass are much more forgiving, load a lot faster and easier, and can sail a 2- or 3-ounce plug far out into the suds. Graphite is lighter, so your arms don't get so tired from casting all night, but they are also expensive—too expensive to be broken when you fall or trip. In many instances, graphite is much

Fish the edge of outcroppings with crashing surf. The rolling waves and turbulent water will draw big fish in to feed. Almost all stripers, no matter what size, like white-water and rough conditions.

too stiff and brittle and is vulnerable if nicked or scratched. Working in a bait shop for the last eight years, I've seen an awful lot of graphite rods come back for warranty work or that have broken while casting or fighting a fish. On the other hand, we see few if any glass rods being returned for those same reasons. Usually when a glass rod comes back it's to have the eyes rewrapped because of wear.

I have nine surf rods in my cellar. Four of them belonged to my father, and the other five are mine. My son has used the same rod as his grandfather, and my grandson has now used what his father, his grandfather and great-grandfather used. I know of no graphite rod that has that type of longevity. Rods made of S-Glass or E-Glass will give you the lightness in weight as well as the toughness needed to survive long years of use in the surf.

The prevailing belief is that you need a rod that is long enough to toss a lure, bait, or jig to Europe on each cast if you're going to have a chance of catching a fish. That is not true at all. The places that those conditions exist are few and far between. Are there places where long casts are necessary most of the time? Of course. Beaches where the cuts and troughs lie far from shore and the area in between is devoid of fish or areas like the Cape Cod Canal, where at times the fish seem to be out in the middle and nowhere else, require long casts. However, most of the time, in most areas, the fish are at your feet and not hundreds of yards out in front of you. Most anglers new to surf fishing make the mistake of fishing farther than where most of the fish are.

When I look back on most of the bigger fish that I caught when surf casting, very few were taken at the end of a long cast and most were hooked 15 to 20 feet from the end of the rod tip. Even when you hook a big fish right after a long cast, it is awfully difficult to get a good hook-set on him. Some would argue that you can make up for this by using braided line, as it has less stretch than mono. That might be true, but as I stated earlier, I don't like braided line for many types of fishing, let alone surf casting, because it is less resistant to abrasion. When surf casting from a nice sandy beach, braided line would be fine, but braid quickly loses its luster around rocks and other obstructions.

Lures and Baits

The same lures will work as effectively from the surf as they will from a boat, so there is no need to go and buy different lures simply because you are fishing from the beach. Even the lure colors will remain the same. Stick to basic white, yellow, black, red and white, and chartreuse, and you'll have most conditions covered.

Remember that you can use surface poppers at night. Whoever said that poppers only work during the day probably didn't fish much or at least didn't ever try out new ideas or techniques. To be fair, even I bought into this one for many years. Then one night while I was fishing a bar with some fellow club members, one guy from New Jersey pulled out a big white popper and began tossing it seaward. Everyone there giggled and made jokes—until he began catching fish one after another. When I asked him why he had decided to use a popper, he answered that he

Here an angler points to stripers chasing bait close to the beach in only inches of water, common when stripers are on small bait. Small soft plastics and flies would work great for these fish. *Joe Manansala photo*

A rod sits in a sand spike on a barren beach. Birds are working over fish close to shore. It's every fisherman's dream to see this. *Joe Manansala photo*

had done this for more than twenty years and found it amazing that I hadn't known about the technique. Shows what I know. Poppers work very well at night when the seas are calm and there is little or no wind. Fished slowly and deliberately, a popper will attract big bass under the cover of darkness when nothing else seems to work.

If you want a big fish from the surf, then fishing with a live eel, live baitfish, or cut bait on the bottom is the way to get one or at least raise the odds in your favor tenfold. (See chapter 9 for tips on how to rig eels and baitfish.) Within the surf-fishing community today there is a prevailing belief that using any bait is somehow cheating. Bait is simply another tool of the trade. Would you try to cut a 2 x 4 with a hammer or drive a nail with a screwdriver? Of course not. What it comes down to is simply using the best tool at the right time and in the right circumstances. Bait has its place in surf fishing, as do plugs, jigs, and flies.

The Best Times to Fish

Tides, wind, and bait movement dictate your success in the surf. When all three elements come together, the fishing will usually be very good. When one or more of these elements is not favorable, the fishing will be slow or not good at all. On average, the number of days that all three of these conditions come together during a season is limited. That is the reason that spending as much time as possible on the water is so critical to success. How many times have you heard that you "should have been here yesterday?" That really does happen. You can miss these conditions by hours or even minutes, and it would appear that there are no fish in the sea. Too many anglers believe that fish tend to feed all the time, every day. This is simply not true. Fish are like people; they only eat when they're hungry.

The front and back sides of storms are good times to fish the surf. The problem is figuring out exactly when that magic time is going to occur. Sometimes it can be hours before or after, sometimes a day, and sometimes only minutes when the fish go on a feeding binge. It can

One sure sign of fish feeding along the beach are baitfish that have been pushed into the surf line and have become trapped on shore. This would certainly be an area you'd have to fish before moving on. *Joe Manansala photo*

This striper fell for a large wooden swimmer fished on a night tide. In the summer, surf anglers should prowl the shoreline after dark. Make sure you know where you are going by visiting the spot during the day and on a low tide.

be localized or occur throughout miles of shoreline. Sometimes it happens totally unexpectedly, as it did during our trip to Block Island in the 1980s (see Chapter 11, A November Storm). The last thing in the world that any of us ever expected was to run into so many fish during that terrible storm.

Many areas have certain wind conditions that turn the fish on. Get to know these areas and visit them frequently to fish those conditions. In other areas it can be a matter of the tide. For instance breachways and river outflows are best fished on dropping water. Rivers will usually be the easiest to figure out, since their rate of flow and the time of dropping water will usually be pretty consistent. Inside of breachways, the tides can be delayed as much as two hours or more from the stated high water levels on the beach side. These are the kind of conditions the surf fisherman needs to learn and adapt to.

Gear and Equipment

You'll need a certain amount of gear to fish the surf effectively and safely. But choose your gear wisely because, unlike boat fishing, you have to carry everything you bring.

Waders

The first item is a good set of waders. There are three types: rubber, neoprene, and breathable. What you choose will depend on the time of the year and the weather. You really don't want to wear rubber or neoprene waders during the middle of the summer or when you have to walk far to the fishing area. You'll wind up sweating and losing some weight. Advancements in clothing technology have brought under-garments to the point that you can now layer beneath your breathable waders and still remain dry, warm, and comfortable. However, if you do not layer properly, breathable waders can be cold and uncomfortable in spring and late fall. You should always wear a wader belt around your waist and make sure it's snug so water has a harder time getting inside your waders.

Rain Pants and Boots

If you fish from a jetty, it's best to wear a pair of rain pants and calf-high boots. That way, if you should have an accident and get

Anyone who wades or fishes from shore needs a good pair of waders. Modern waders are high tech, and will keep you warm and dry through the seasons as long as you layer properly. *River and Riptide Anglers photo*

swept off the jetty, you don't have to worry about your waders filling up with water and dragging you under. It's also much easier to maneuver on the rocks with rain pants and boots than it is with waders on.

Life Vest

The new type of inflatable life vests that fit around your neck and waist are lightweight, comfortable, and easy to inflate if you should go into the water. Some inflate automatically, and others require the angler to pull a valve-release. In either case, if you fish from rocks where it's easy to get knocked down, a life vest is a good investment.

Surf Bag

Surf bags are almost a necessity for carrying the lures and other items that you may need. You don't want a bag so big that you wind up carrying everything but the kitchen sink. Learn to fish a few lures effectively and properly instead of carrying more than you'll ever use. Its just extra weight that will tire you out from carrying it long distances.

Many types of lure bags are available. Most go over your shoulder and some fit around your waist. You can also make your own with old Army-Navy surplus bags. Cut thin PVC tubing and insert it into the bag to hold your lures.

Headlamp

When fishing at night you'll need a good headlamp to safely find your way out and back in. Lights today are not only small and compact, but they are bright and waterproof as well. One model I like from Inova is small and it has seven different LCD light combinations as well as a distress and SOS signal in case you get into trouble. The battery will last almost an entire season of hard use. These lights are so good that we carry one on our boat as well. I've used the signaling feature on this light in dense fog and had other boats spot it from a mile or more away. They are somewhat expensive but worth every penny in terms of peace of mind.

School bass feeding on small bait just off the beach. Not all fish will be big ones but usually there are bigger fish somewhere close by. *Joe Manansala photo*

Cutting Pliers

You'll need a good set of cutting pliers for removing hooks from fish and cutting lines. You may also need it for removing hooks from someone. If you hook yourself and are alone, you'll be glad that you have pliers with you. There is nothing worse than having a hook in your hand with a fish on the end of it and not being able to get that extra weight off, especially when it's flipping and flopping.

Sharpening Stone

A small sharpening stone for touching up hook points is also good to carry. I happen to like the model made by Luhr Jensen and Sons. It's a simple file about 7 inches long with a yellow handle you can easily grasp.

Birds and bent rods can only mean one thing—big bass are in the surf and feeding.

Wading Staff

In some areas, guys now carry wading staffs like those freshwater anglers use. Wading staffs are made from high-tech materials and are light in weight as well as strong. Folstaf makes one of the finer wading staffs, and they are collapsible to make carrying them easier. Shallow-water rocky bars covered with rock and weed can be difficult to walk over and keep your balance, especially if there is big surf rolling in over the bar. A wading staff makes going in and out that much easier. Attach it to the back of your wader belt when you start fishing, and it will remain out of the way.

CHAPTER 11

A NOVEMBER STORM

THE DATE WAS NOVEMBER 20, 1986, and we were headed to the fabled fishing shores of Block Island, Rhode Island, for what we hoped would be a week of fabulous surf casting. What we didn't know on the morning of our departure was what Mother Nature had planned for our journey over there.

John Jollie, Steve Catterall, Joe McCary, Rich Colagiovanni, and I had made this trip many times before to fish some of the most fertile and productive waters that existed during that time in history. The island was famous all across New England (and still is) for its ability to attract and hold big striped bass in amazing numbers during the fall run, which lasts to the beginning of December. This was during a time when fish were measured not in numbers or inches but in hundreds and thousands of pounds.

At 5 A.M. on the morning of the 20th, the five of us met for breakfast at Snoppy's Diner, a local restaurant where many anglers ate before departing on the many fishing charters that left out of Point Judith. After sitting down and getting our coffee, Richard asked if anyone had

Big wind and high surf can mean excellent fishing, especially in the fall. The beginning and back sides of fall storms can trigger good fishing. Knowing when to be there is the key to catching more fish.

heard the latest marine weather forecast. We all answered no, but he had. "They're calling for winds out of the southeast, at 35 to 45 miles per hour and gusting to 60," he said. We immediately wondered if the ferry crossing would be postponed or even canceled. At that time of the year, cancellations were common. We had already spent a lot of money on renting a house on the island for the week, and losing all that money didn't sit well with any of us.

We finished our breakfast and then headed to Galilee, in Point Judith, where we parked our trucks in the ferry loading line and headed to the ticket office. It was 7 A.M. and the wind was easily blowing twenty-five knots already. We asked the ticket office girl if the boat was going to make the morning run. She said they hadn't yet decided, and that they were going to wait until 8 A.M. before they made a final decision. During the hour we had to kill and sweat it out, four more vehicles arrived, likely island residents returning home from business on the mainland, three big trucks loaded with building supplies for contractors on the island, and a few passengers who were on their way over to the island for a visit.

As we were waiting by our trucks, I looked up at the sky. It was gunmetal gray, with big, thick, charcoal-colored clouds set in a patchwork across the sky. Beneath them were long, wispy gray mares' tails moving swiftly below the billowing clouds above. I then turned to Joe, who was standing next to me, and asked him if he had ever seen such an ominous looking sky before. With a quick gaze skyward, he simply said, "No, I haven't. This does not look good at all."

At 8:40 A.M. we were told that the ferry was going to make the run after all. We drove our trucks on, and then we went upstairs to the passengers' lounge on the second deck. We all reassured ourselves by noting that at least this was a new, straight-out-of-the-box, triple-decker boat. It was massive compared to the older ferry. We each assured the other that we'd have no problems whatsoever and that they must know what they were doing, as they had made this run in bad weather many times.

At 9:00 A.M. the ferry blew her whistle, backed out of her berth, and headed up the channel away from the harbor of refuge and toward the open ocean. As we cleared what's known as the short wall, we could see the long, black, rock formations that made up the East Wall breakwater in front of Point Judith Lighthouse, as well as the outside center wall.

What we also saw, however, was somewhat unnerving, if not downright frightening. We could see the windswept waves being pushed and driven by the high winds right into those immoveable rocky structures. When it met with this mass of granite, the water exploded into the air with the sound of mortar rounds exploding. Huge sheets of white foam and water were sent 10 to 12 feet skyward, and the loud crashing sound roared and echoed, even at a mile or more away. It was now evident what we'd be dealing with once we reached the outside of the harbor. And we had a full 12 miles of open ocean to cross before we reached the safety of the island.

A quarter-mile out from the last breakwater, we overheard two of the mates say, "I think we might have made a big mistake today." Joe was standing next to me and asked if I had heard what they had just said. I simply nodded my head in agreement. "Jesus," said Joe, "I knew we should have stayed on land. I just knew it!" But it was already too late. The captain had committed himself to making the run, and it would have been suicide to try and turn that big square box of a boat in seas of this magnitude. There was no place to go except toward the island.

It wasn't long before the island's residents on board, as well as those few passengers who had also decided to make the trip, were all leaning over the rail and losing their breakfasts. Two became so nervous and upset they actually passed out and were put on the floor inside the passengers lounge to roll around on the deck as the boat rolled up and down and from side to side.

With each dip of the bow, the water broke and rushed over the lower deck. The captain tried as hard as he could to veer the ship in a quartering fashion so as to not take any broadside hits from the monstrous waves, which were now 12 to 15 feet high and building. When he did misjudge, the water heaved skyward and sent water up and above the third deck of the ferry. Here we were on a three-story boat, and green water was coming over the top.

For the first time in my life on the water, I was scared. The last time I had said more Hail Marys and Our Fathers, I was curled up inside a

In our 4 x 4 overlooking Black Rock Cove on Block Island to see if it was fishable that day. This area of Block Island was famous for giving up big stripers in the fall and the spring.

foxhole in the jungle. This was serious stuff, and we all knew it. We had all been on the water for years and had been caught in all types of bad weather. We had always dealt with it and we'd always made it home, but this was different. This was *Perfect Storm* stuff, and we were caught right in the middle of it with nowhere to go or to hide.

The battering continued unabated for the next two hours. Wave after wave rolled toward the boat as if they were going to roll right up and inside it at any minute. On each one we all held our breath and on each one our hearts stopped for a split second. Finally, the island came into view. Maybe, just maybe, we would make it alive.

Then, about 2 miles or so out from the island we heard this loud bang. A one-inch safety chain that was holding one of the big trucks secure snapped. This truck was loaded with rebar and secured to the deck so it wouldn't move. The big problem now was that this truck was also the last in line and right next to the big drop-down door that served as the ramp on and off the boat. If that truck slid back and hit that door, forcing it open, we'd likely sink before making it to the island. The mates worked frantically to re-secure the truck with additional chain, twice getting knocked down by waves going over the bottom deck. We stood above watching this happen, and no one uttered one word. I don't think anyone knew exactly what to say anyway.

The ferry finally made it close enough to get within the protection of the island, as it provided a shield against the wind and high seas. My handheld VHF radio was tuned to the NOAA weather station, which was now issuing warnings to mariners to seek safe harbor quickly because of the storm's sudden intensity. "Winds are blowing steadily at 45 knots, gusting to 60 and 65 knots. Seas are 12 to 15 feet and climbing; heavy rain is approaching, with the possibility of changing over to snow later in the afternoon." Winds were forecast to switch to the north/northeast, setting this storm up to be a classic Nor'easter, which during the summer months would be classified as a hurricane.

When the ferry finally docked, the ramp was lowered and we drove our trucks off quickly. I pulled into the first parking spot that I could find, got out of my truck, and kissed the tar as if it were a beautiful woman, while offering thanks to God for sparing my miserable life. The 12-mile run over to the island usually takes 50 minutes or so; ours had taken 3 hours and 27 minutes.

We then headed to our house to unload our gear and figure out what we'd do next. The conversation over there revolved around our hair-raising ride and how we had survived without getting sick as everyone else had—the one thing we were all proud of. Although I'll freely admit that I'd come as close to blowing my lunch as I had ever had, I think the sheer terror of the ride kept it from actually happening.

Steve was the first one to say, "Okay, what are we going to do now, just sit here and talk? Or are we going to go fishing, which is why we came here in the first place? I don't want to think about that ride over any longer."

Up until that point, I don't believe anyone even considered what we'd do next. Joe then suggested that we go and check the back side of the island, which would likely be in the lee of the wind, and hopefully the big seas as well. We quickly agreed and headed to Dory's Cove on

Rich Colagiovanni and Steve Catterall casting at the legendary Southwest Bar on Block Island. This bar has given up thousands of big bass over the years to surf casters from all up and down the coast. Its natural features make it an area where big bass like to feed.

the opposite side of the island. On the way there, the rain began falling hard.

Upon arriving, we parked our trucks, unracked our surf rods, and started to make our way toward the small path through the bushes that leads down to the water and the cove. The path itself was now a minia-ture river moving mud, stones, and litter toward the rocky beach from all the rain that was falling. It also made for slippery walking; John and Joe slipped and ripped their waders in the process. Rich was the first one down the path and through the bushes. He had only walked about ten feet beyond the opening when he stopped dead in his tracks. It was now 2:45 P.M. and raining even harder. The rest of us cleared the hedges out into the open and froze as well. What lay before us, to the right, to the left, and for as far as we could see, were breaking bass in untold numbers. Instead of waves and wind turning the sea's surface white, it was the stripers, as they fed like we have never seen before or since. This was at a time in the mid-1980s, when the striped bass were at their lowest numbers, so what lay before us seemed surely to be every striped bass that remained alive in the ocean.

For what seemed like an eternity but was probably no more than a minute or two, we stood fixated in amazement and awe by what we were witnessing. Maybe it was because of our recent ride over and the hazardous experience we just had, or maybe it was just sheer shock at what was happening right before our eyes. Once reality set in, our needlefish lures quickly went seaward into the mega-blitz of feeding striped bass.

Rich was the first to hook up when a fish of about 25 pounds inhaled his lure as it hit the water. Then Joe scored with a 35-pounder. Then it was Steve's turn; a fish just over 40 pounds swallowed his green needlefish right at his feet. As this was going on, John answered with two fish at once on the same lure. One was 15 pounds and the second was a bit over 20. And on and on it went: one hour, two hours, three hours. It was now 5:45 P.M., it was dark, and still the bite did not let up. It was nonstop, fish after fish, the likes of which we had never experienced.

Yet in all that time, I still hadn't caught or hooked a single fish, and I was frustrated beyond belief. At one point, I had raised my rod and reel over my head, ready to slam it into the rocks, when suddenly John grabbed my arm and pulled it down and said, "What in hell are you doing?"

"I can't take it anymore," I answered. "I can't take one more minute of this."

I had a brand new Lamiglas 10½-foot surf rod with a brand new Ambassador 7000 casting reel, and before he stopped me, I was totally committed to smashing it on the rocks without even thinking about the cost. Stripers can have that effect on you, especially when you can see them at your feet and you can't catch any. I had tried every trick I knew to get a fish to hit, and nothing had worked.

"Take it easy and have a cigarette." John suggested. "You know this kind of stuff happens as well as anybody. It could be me, Joe, Rich, or Steve tomorrow or the day after. It's part of the game. Now get your head back on straight," he ordered me.

I knew he was right, even though I didn't want to admit it. Between the four of them, they had already accounted for somewhere in the neighborhood of 200 fish from 18 to 44 pounds, and I hadn't caught so much as a school bass. All I had accomplished was to lose six new plugs and create seven

John Jollie with one of many big fish taken that week. The Coast Guard station at Block Island is in the backround, and the channel leading to the salt pond is close by. This channel holds big fish during the fall.

or eight serious backlashes. They were all right here around me, next to me, behind me, in front of me, and I hadn't even gotten a hit. How much did they expect one guy to take?

At 6:45 P.M. we were still fishing. The weather had now gone from a pelting, driving rain, to a cold, wet snow. All five of us were soaked.

A much younger Jim White holds a nice Block Island striper taken from shore, 1986. Big fish like this were the norm back then, but small school bass were almost impossible to find.

But at least my run of bad luck was beginning to change. I had now landed seven or eight fish in the high twenties to high thirties, and I was beginning to feel a lot more confident. The wet snow ran down the backs of our necks as it melted from our hats and rain gear and found its way into every opening on our body. The wetness was bone-chilling in the darkness, but we continued to fish.

Steve was next to me when I heard him shout that he had a good fish on and needed help. I quickly moved closer to see if I could help him out as he tried to pump the big fish closer. As the fish came into the wash, we put our lights on her to see how big she was. As the wave curled and rolled toward shore, it picked her up and pushed her close to the shoreline, where I shoved my hand down her throat and into her gills. "Nice fish old man. I think you got yourself a fifty here," I told Steve.

Steve took the fish and dragged it up onto the beach and away from the surf line. He then began working on unhooking the fish from the big swimmer it had eaten. It was then that I heard him scream to me once again that he needed help. I went over to see what the problem was, and the only thing that I saw in the light of my headlight was blood. Not the fish's blood, but Steve's. As he'd attempted to remove the last treble hook from the big fish, it flipped one last time and sent the trebles deep into his right hand.

Well, it was finally over. I went to tell John and Rich that we needed to get Steve to a doctor to remove the hook embedded in his hand. Besides, we were tired, totally wet from head to toe, and we hadn't eaten anything since 5 A.M. We returned to the trucks with Steve's fish in tow and his hand bandaged and bleeding. When we arrived, Joe noticed he had a flat tire. It had a huge screw in it. We now had to change the tire in the snow on a slippery, muddy, snow-covered parking area. Was it all ever going to end?

After we'd gotten Steve taken care of, we were all sitting in the living room back at the house having a few beers and looking back over the day's events. Rich was sitting there in his quiet, laid-back, backwoods way (he could have been Daniel Boone in another life) and quietly said: "You know, this is going to be one day the five of us will never forget as long as we live. We took a boat ride in 20-foot seas, damned near died in the process, found the biggest school of stripers any of us has ever seen in our lives or ever will see again, and caught countless numbers of fish (except for Jim). It rained, it snowed, the wind blew, we got a flat tire, we ripped two pairs of waders, lost dozens of plugs, had to find a doctor in the middle of the night for Steve on a godforsaken island, and all in one fifteen-hour period. I was just sitting here wondering what everyone else out there did today."

As were the rest of us.

CHAPTER 12

FLY-ROD STRIPERS

A ROUND 1990 I started successfully targeting large stripers on the fly in Rhode Island's Narragansett Bay, and I believe that I was among the first to do so. Or, if others were doing it, they certainly kept it quiet. One thing that aided me in this quest was my previous big-fish experience and knowledge of their movements within the bay, as well as an understanding of the key times during the season when they were most likely to be available. We concentrated our time and effort on areas we knew would hold or had the potential to hold big fish. On some occasions it worked perfectly, and on many others it didn't work at all. That's the way fishing for this creature is—there are more bad days than good.

During that time period, which was right after the striper crash of the late 1970s and early 1980s, big fish were not all that common in our waters, and on many days we resorted to fishing for school bass, which seemed to be limitless. All my experience with big fish occurred in the 1960s and 1970s before the crash. It was my good fortune to have fished when there were loads of big fish, so I got plenty of

Lefty Kreh casts a tight loop like no one else. He makes it look so easy that it's embarrassing at times. You'll catch more fish with good casting technique. *Mike Laptew photo*

practice. After that time, trying to gain the knowledge of big-bass habits was tough since there weren't many big fish around. It's not easy to correct your mistakes when you're trying to catch the last remaining fish in the ocean.

At that time, I fished from a Florida-style flats boat, which not only allowed me to get into skinny water but also to stand on the poling platform and spot fish. In the spring, our waters are clear and do not get off-colored until warmer weather arrives or if there's been a lot of rain and runoff from the rivers. The biggest learning experience I ever had was standing on that poling platform and watching things unfold before my eyes.

Flies and Equipment

Though big bass will eat 2- to 4-inch flies at times, most of the time they prefer something bigger. If you are going to target big fish, then use big flies—flies that are 7 to 12 inches—that imitate the biggest bait available to them at the time. In the spring, herring, squid, and menhaden patterns are often the best choices. In early summer, bunker, squid, and eel flies work well. At night, nothing beats an eel pattern fished just below or right on the surface when the water is calm.

Flies that move or push the water when on the surface are also good. You can make them float by using wool to form a body and then dipping the body in a coating like Softex. Spun deer-hair bodies can also add bulk and flotation to a big fly. By using long, thin hackle feathers, you can add length and a lot of movement in the tail, which attracts bass. Big Deceiver-type flies, including big Bucktail Deceivers, are also good choices. If you tie them bulky and fat, they will swim closer to the surface.

The original *White Ghost* was an Action Craft flats boat. Flats boats are excellent platforms from which to fish and have few obstructions to catch your fly line.

The White Ghost Squid is simple and easy to tie. It is a good fly in spring and fall when the squid are running.

WHITE GHOST SQUID

Hook:	#3/0-4/0 Matzuo O'Shaughnessy
Thread:	White monocord; black for the head
Tentacles:	Long white saddle hackles, three or four on each side turned outward, dot with permanent marker
Flash:	Pearl Krystal Flash
Body:	Purple Bodi-Braid wrapped over a small glass rattle
Head:	Pearl E-Z Body about half the length of the hook shank (coated with epoxy), white saddle hackle spun at the eye
Eyes:	Red and black doll eyes coated with epoxy

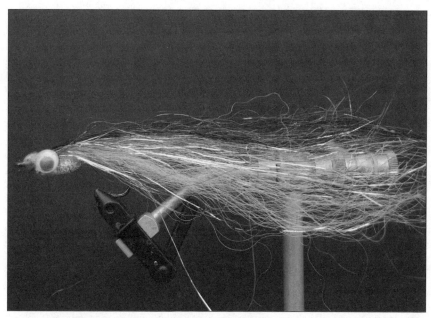

A 9-inch-long White Ghost Herring fly with big doll eyes and rattles in the body. This is one of my go-to patterns during the early part of the spring when river herring are ascending the rivers to spawn.

WHITE GHOST HERRING

Hook:	#3/0-4/0 Matzuo O'Shaughnessy
Tail:	White yak hair 6 to 9 inches long covered with yellow, green, and blue yak hair with pearl Krystal Flash mixed in
Body:	Short piece of E-Z Body with glass rattle underneath
Top:	Black and dark green yak hair, mixed
Eyes:	Yellow and black doll eyes
Head:	Red monocord

The Rhody Flat Wing is popular in the Northeast for striper fishing. This fly has accounted for a lot of big bass over the years and should be included in your fly box.

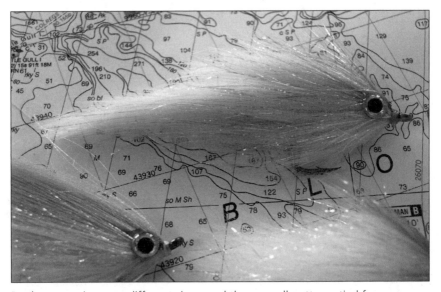

Bunker come in many different sizes, and these small patterns tied from synthetic hair are easy to tie and shape to match the naturals. *River and Riptide Anglers photo*

Capt. Jim White and Dan Blanton admire a fish Blanton took on a Crease Fly in shallow water at 11 A.M. It was late September and the fish were feeding on small peanut bunker. *Mike Laptew photo*

When fishing during the daytime, the same type of patterns will work, but make sure you also try the Clouser Deep Minnow and the big Clouser/Kreh Half and Half. This latter fly, tied as long as possible, has taken more big bass for me than all the others combined. There's just something about this fly that big stripers find irresistible. When fishing the flats, you'll want your fly to sink a bit slower than normal due to the shallowness of the water, so big flies should be tied sparse and wide. When using flies such as Clouser Deep Minnows, I usually use small weighted eyes so it doesn't sink as quickly. The fish need time to spot the fly, and you only have a couple of feet of water to make that happen. Mix up your retrieve to find what the fish are looking for on that particular day.

Like the old saying goes, "Don't bring a knife to a gunfight." When targeting big stripers, use a 10- or 11-weight rod with a floating or intermediate line. Not only will a heavier rod allow you to cast the larger flies more easily into the wind, even in the shallow water of a sand flat,

Fly rods from 9- to 11-weight will suffice for most of the shallow-water fishing you will encounter. I like 10-weights. You are prepared for large fish, but if you run into small fish you can land them quickly and get them back in the water with little stress. This gets you back in the big-fish ballgame quickly. *River and Riptide Anglers photo*

Fly reels come in all sizes, shapes, and materials. Choose one that has a good drag and one that will stand up to the rigors of saltwater fishing. Make sure you maintain your reels to keep them in top working order. *River and Riptide Anglers photo*

a big fish will run hard for the nearest deep water it can find. It's much better to stop it on the flat than to let it get into deep water.

There are lots of different styles, sizes, and prices of fly reels. Reels currently available range from inexpensive graphite models all the way to machined aluminum models that go for a month's mortgage payment. You do not need to spend a lot of money on a good reel for striper fishing. I know guys who have used the Scientific Anglers System I or II reels for years and have had no problems with them, and they can be purchased for a couple hundred bucks.

The reel must have a good drag and the capacity to hold about 200 yards of backing. Anything more than that is overkill. Tales of long-distance runs by monster bass make for exciting stories, but they aren't plausible. I've caught many big bass in my day and been present when many big fish were caught, and in all honesty, I don't recall any fish running nonstop for a hundred yards. In reality, fish over 40 pounds don't run that far at all. They tire very quickly. It's no different than me

Silicone flies were made popular by Bob Popovics and have gained a good reputation for fooling large stripers. *River and Riptide Anglers photo*

trying to outdistance my grandson in a race. Chances are, I'm going to collapse long before reaching the finish line. His young legs would surely win out, and fish are no different. The hardest fighters are the bass in the teens, twenties, and thirties. The only reasons a fish might run a long distance would be an improper drag setting, a nonfunctioning drag, bad fishing technique, or a combination of all three.

I constantly check my drags for smoothness, and I tune and set them with a good scale so I know exactly how many pounds of pressure I can exert before reaching the breaking strength of the leader or backing. (I do this with spinning and casting reels as well.) Knowing for sure how much pressure your line is capable of handling is critical when pursuing big stripers. I also routinely clean and lube my reels, and loosen the drag when I am not using them for a long period of time. If you leave your drag turned down tight over a long period of time, the drag washers will become deformed and eventually be rendered useless.

As I began to target bigger fish, my methods and tactics evolved as well. One of the first things I did was change the pound-test strength of the leaders and tippet material I was using. I stopped using tapered leaders of 10- to 15-pound-test and instead went to leaders from 25- to 40-pound-test. The more rocks in an area, the higher the pound-test we'd use. Not only did it work, but it allowed us to land some really big fish that we would probably have otherwise lost.

Morgan Wood shows a nice midsize striper on a fly taken at sunrise. Not all fish will or can be monsters, but they are fun nonetheless.

When I was poling fly anglers from a flats skiff, I began to see a pattern developing where the angler would hook a nice fish (say, in the mid to high teens) and, with few exceptions, quickly lose it. This happened so many times that I began to wonder just what was going on. I knew that not all of the anglers I had were that bad at fly fishing, so it had to be something else.

Then one day, right up close to the boat, a client was getting ready to lift his line out of the water for the next cast, when a 20-pound fish came out of nowhere and ate his fly. When the angler set the hook, the fish immediately turned sideways, parallel to the line and the leader. That leader was now right alongside the striper's body, rubbing against all those big scales, spines, and gill plates. When the fish lunged to free himself and make his run, the leader popped like a rifle shot. When I asked the client what pound-test leader and tippet he was using, he said 12 pounds. From that day forward, any client who wanted a big fish never had anything less than a 25-pound-test leader on the end of his line.

Using a heavy leader accomplishes two things. First, when you hook a small fish, you can boat it quickly, unhook it, and get it back in the water fast. This is not only good for the fish, but gives you

Lefty takes time out to get his knots and leader tied correctly. Doing it right the first time can mean the difference between a big fish and no fish. The Line Tamer in the background is useful for controlling your fly line. *Mike Laptew photo*

more time to fish for the larger ones. Second, when a big fish does come knocking, you have something of substance between you and the fish's body and any underwater obstacles it might try to wrap around. Big fish head for the nearest rock, bar, ledge, shell bed, or other bottom debris that it can find to rub out the fly stuck in its jaw as quickly as it can.

I use both monofilament and fluorocarbon leader material. Early in the season, stripers aren't that leader shy, and they're also feeding heavily after taking the winter off. At this time, I tend to use mono because the fact that it is slightly more visible than fluorocarbon doesn't matter. As the season progresses, I'll switch to fluorocarbon leaders as anglers put pressure on the fish. A tip: Don't wet or spit on fluorocar-

Nick Curcione holds a 24-pound striper taken on one of his menhaden creations. Nick had noticed and cast to some nervous water, and was rewarded with this fish.

bon when attaching it to your main line or your lure. Fluorocarbon is already naturally slippery, and wetting it will only cause your knot to slip more easily.

When you decide to pursue big stripers with fly tackle, you really can't leave anything to chance. Regularly check all leaders and knots for frays, nicks, and wind knots to reduce the possibility of anything slipping or breaking while a big fish in on the line. Remember that your leader and subsequent connections to the line and backing are the only connection you have to the fish. If one or more of these fails, the ballgame is over.

When fishing some of the deeper areas, such as bridge abutments and deeper channel banks, you'll often need a sinking line or lead-core shooting head to get the fly deeper. These areas are likely best fished with a weighted fly as well, as there is some current to deal with. You can sink your fly deeply by mending line upstream to allow the rig time to sink without drag.

Fly Casting

Once you have your gear and flies ready, the next thing to do is to practice your casting. Then practice, practice, and practice some more. Fly fishing isn't like spin fishing or bait casting. Once you learn how to use a spinning or casting reel, you don't forget. With fly casting, if you fish today and then you don't go for weeks or a month or more, you almost wind up going back to square one. Until you are proficient with the long rod and have developed your timing and casting stroke, you should practice as much as possible, especially with big flies. The better you can make that 50- to 70-foot cast accurately, the better your chances will be of fulfilling your dream of landing a monster striper on a fly rod. In my guide business, the most common limiting factor is anglers' inability to make long, accurate casts with a big fly.

To cast large flies, often in the wind, you will have to master your double-haul. There are many great instructional dvds and books out there, but none are better than Lefty Kreh's new book on casting, *Cast-*

By making sure your tackle is ready and capable of handling a big fish, you up the odds of landing it. I've seen many a nice striper hooked and lost on fly tackle that wasn't set up to handle the task at hand.

ing with Lefty Kreh. In that book, Lefty not only breaks down the double-haul but also explains how to casting sinking lines and shooting heads, which you will need to know how to do if you want to fish your flies in deep water or fast currents.

Also, don't just practice your distance casting. Being able to cast quickly and accurately will often serve you better. Learn to cast with a minimal number of false-casts and practice casting at targets in your

Jerry Gibbs plays a big striper on his fly rod in shallow water while on *White Ghost 2*. Sand flats can be excellent fly-fishing areas in the spring.

backyard to improve your accuracy. As Lefty recommends, practice with large, weighted flies—like the ones that you will be fishing—rather than a little piece of yarn.

Another thing that I have learned by fishing with Lefty over the years is that good casting is effortless and efficient. Lefty Kreh taught me to use my rod and line to make a longer, smoother cast with less effort. Some guys jump and jerk all over the place when casting, believing these extra body gyrations will get their line and fly out farther. They won't.

While some situations require a long cast to catch fish, most of the large fish I've caught or seen caught were hooked and fought very close to the angler. That does not mean that you do not have to know how to make a long, accurate cast, but the longer the cast and the farther away you hook a big fish, the more likely it is that you'll either miss him or lose him because of a weak hook-set.

Boat position plays a critical role in fly casting. When fishing the flats, you want to have the sun at your back if possible so you can get

Playing a big fish requires patience and skill, especially when they get close to the boat, where most fish are lost. This is no time to be rushing to get the fish in, as it probably still has at least one more big run left.

a better view of the bottom and any fish cruising the flat. Next, make sure the wind is behind you or at least quartering so your casting is easier and more accurate. If you can see the fish, accuracy will be extremely important, and many times you'll only get that one shot at a big fish. Chances are if you see him, he can also see you. When using spinning or conventional tackle this isn't as critical since you can pretty much toss a lure or jig in almost any direction, even if it's windy, without sacrificing too much accuracy. You normally don't have that option or convenience when using a fly rod.

Learn to back cast, especially when fishing from a boat. It will help also in dealing with the wind when it's too strong.

Someone once asked me at a seminar whether fighting the wind or being blinded by the sun was worse, because sometimes the wind and the sun don't cooperate for you. When that happens, and it often does, I'll go with being able to cast easier and give up trying to spot the fish. You can see a million fish on a flat, but you need to be able to get a good cast to them.

Playing Big Fish

I learned a lot about how to fight fish from Nick Curcione, who pioneered the art of fly fishing off the long-range boats in southern California over thirty years ago and was one of the first to take big pelagic fish on a fly from those boats. After his arrival here in New England, he and I became close friends, as he only lived about an hour's drive away from me.

I recall one time when we were fishing for school tuna using a Thomas & Thomas Horizon 14-weight fly rod with a Tibor fly reel and one of his shooting-head systems. He boated and beat those school tuna faster than anyone I'd ever previously seen do before by pulling against the direction the fish was swimming to confuse it and keeping the line and rod low to the water. When we applied those same down-and-dirty tactics to fighting stripers, our ratio of big fish hooked to landed shot up by almost 65 percent. High sticking, when your rod is arched in a big C shape, only applies pressure with the rod tip, and that part of the rod can't apply much pressure at all. By keeping the rod low and minimizing the bend, you fight the fish more with the butt of the rod. That combined with pulling left when the fish goes right, and pulling right when the fish runs left, tires it very quickly. Pressure him, confuse him, use the rod and the reel's drag to your advantage, and don't stop until the fish is at the boat or at your feet.

Lefty Kreh, one of the masters of fighting big fish, taught me a neat trick to deal with tangles that has helped me land some big stripers. When you have a knot or tangle in your line and a fish is pulling on the other end, you should turn your rod upside down. This allows the line to easily pass through the guides without getting caught, and you can still fight and land the fish without snapping your line. This simple trick has saved me many, many big stripers from being lost or breaking off, especially when fishing at night when tangles become a much bigger problem.

But even when you do everything right, sometimes landing the fish of a lifetime is not meant to be. One of the biggest striped bass on fly I have seen was hooked by a doctor from Connecticut while we were fishing a big flat adjacent to a local town beach. On the flat's eastern shore, huge rock formations rose above the bottom about 2 or 3 feet and were surrounded by sand. The area was also known for holding migrating alewives during the spring. The doctor was tossing a 10-inch herring pattern that I had tied the previous night.

As we approached the rock formations, two huge shadows moved from one rock to the next. Both of us saw them at the same time, and we were amazed at their size. From the poling platform, I was instructing him which way the fish were facing and where he should place his first cast. He made a perfect cast, landing his fly about 2 feet beyond and in front of the two big fish. When he moved the fly 2 or 3 feet beyond those rocks, one of the fish turned and slammed it. When he set the hook, the fish took off for the middle of the bay.

After thirty minutes or so, the doctor was still messing with this fish, and I began to think that the longer this fight went on, the higher the probability that we were going to lose it. About five minutes later, the fish was getting closer to the boat and tiring. I grabbed my Boga Grip and leaned over the side of the boat as far as I could with my chest almost in the water. I then reached for the striper's jaw with the Boga and came about 1/16 of an inch from locking onto it. But the hook just came free. It didn't break or bend, it simply came out of the fish's mouth, and the fish swam away.

Use clear fly lines when possible in shallow water. They are much less visible to the fish.

It's hard to say which one of us were more upset with what had just happened, but I remember feeling like the world had been ripped from beneath me. That fish was all of 50 pounds and then some. I'd seen a lot of big fish in my time, and this one was huge. I've never seen another like it since then nor hooked one like it on a fly rod. Did the doctor do something wrong? I don't think so. Sometimes you win and sometimes you lose. That's what fishing is about.

Opposite: Tom Fusco with a 34-pound striper taken in a shallow back cove on a herring fly, which is an excellent spring pattern for big stripers.

Night Fishing

One other advantage we had when we started fly fishing for big shallow-water stripers was that we were willing to fish after dark in prime areas. Since we had already fished these areas using other methods, it was a logical transition. Fly casting after dark took a little getting used to, which is probably one reason why many fly anglers still do not go out at night.

Night fishing offers the fly fisher a whole new range of sounds and sensations while chasing big stripers. The water at night is normally a dark, empty place—devoid of boats and people. Big fish will move into rivers, creeks, and up onto flats under the cover of darkness, as well as into rocky shoreline areas. Try to select an evening close to a new moon when there is little or no wind and a rising tide.

I recommend using a floating line since it is easier to lift, control, and cast. Since you'll be fishing in shallow water, getting deep isn't that

A beautiful, big striper that ate a chartreuse-and-white Lefty's Deceiver just after daybreak in only inches of water. Being there early, beaching the boat, and wading quietly along the shoreline where the fish were feeding were the keys to catching this one.

Capt. Jim White displays a 30-pound bass caught during a spring worm hatch. By using big flies at this time, you can find some big fish feeding alongside the smaller ones.

much of a concern. The second thing I'd recommend is using a Line Tamer basket for your loose fly line when you are fishing from a boat. Line on the deck at night has a way of causing a lot of headaches. You can also use a tall plastic laundry basket with a sandbag in the bottom to keep it upright. I personally don't care for the waist-mounted stripping baskets that are popular. The reason is that my arms are too long. With my 35-inch reach, the basket is always in an awkward position when I'm trying to place the line inside it. I have to wear it so low that it winds up falling down my legs. But many people rely on them when fishing in the surf.

The size and shape of a fly is more important than its color or the exact imitation of baitfish.

Another tip is to tie a small nail knot in your fly line at the point where your line hand typically is when you lift the line out of the water to make the next cast. When you're stripping in line in the dark, as the line passes through your fingers, you'll feel the knot and know you can now lift, haul, and throw.

CHAPTER 13

CONVENTIONAL TACKLE

THE ONE THING you learn quickly when you guide is which gear is good and which is a waste of money. Though I am a Quantum Tackle and Fin-Nor pro staff member, I was using that gear before offered those positions. Before that, I was strictly a Penn reel guy for almost thirty-five years. I also have had the opportunity to test other rods and reels in my writing career of well over twenty-five years. I'm often asked to try new gear and give my professional opinion regarding its ability to perform. So I get to see and test a lot of tackle.

Many large fish are lost due to equipment failure, and one of the most important aspects of being a successful angler is taking care of your tackle and checking it often. Watching Shaw Grigsby prepare his equipment and the effort and time he put into it was eye opening. He changed his line after each time we fished. He constantly cut back his line or leader after one or two fish and retied his lure. He constantly checked his drag to make sure it wasn't sticking or locked up. He sharpened each hook every time he changed baits. He did this quickly and

An assortment of conventional, or casting, reels. The Quantum CBC-30, the Garcia 6500, the Penn 975, and Garcia's Boss Chrome all have excellent drag systems and have stood up to the rigors of fishing in the brine.

efficiently, almost as if it were mechanical. He caught some really nice fish on light tackle during our shoot and not once did he get busted

off from a weak connection or bad knot. Paying attention to all these seemingly small details can make the difference between landing and catching a big fish or wishing you had taken the extra time to do it as you watch a big one swim away.

Quantum's CB-20 trolling reel and the Cabo heavy-action bait rod are good choices when fishing with big live menhaden and targeting monster stripers. This outfit gives you the control and the power to muscle in big bass.

Casting Reels

You need a well-built reel that will stand up to the rigors of a saltwater environment. For general conditions with small- to medium-size lures, a narrow-spool bait-casting reel will cast farther, faster, and more accurately than models with a wide spool. The Quantum PTLW-30 casting reel is compact, lightweight, and it can hold more than enough line to get the job done. It also has a terrific drag system.

Medium-size reels include the popular Shimano Calcutta 400; the Abu Garcia 5000 and 6000 series; and the Quantum IRON IR4X, which is presently being upgraded to compete with other high-end reels on the market. All are capable of holding at least 200 yards of 20-pound mono (plenty for stripers), and all are good for tossing live eels or large lures and plastics.

Even small casting reels that are well built, tough, and strong like this Quantum CBC-30 will handle big fish. The Quantum Iron IR4X, Shimano's Calcutta, and Garcia's 5000 and 6000 series are all well-built casting reels.

For larger casting reels, the Abu Garcia 7000 or 9000 work great, as does the Shimano 700, or the Quantum 30, which has no level-wind mechanism across the bar frame. Some guys like that style and some don't. Another addition to the line of large casting reels is the Fin-Nor IGFA Class 12 or 16. All of these reels are excellent for live bait, jigging, trolling, or any situations where you need the extra power of a bigger reel.

Spinning Reels

In my professional opinion, the Quantum Cabo and Boca series and the Fin-Nor Mega-Lite and IGFA Class 8 and 12 are the only spinning reels you will ever need. The Quantum Cabo reels have a magnetic bail mechanism, so there is no spring to break or stretch; an almost unbreakable titanium bail arm; and stainless-steel spool, handle, and main shaft. They have a six-layer protective coating, the same type as on Mercury outboards, to guard against saltwater corrosion and a guaranteed 24-hour turnaround time on any factory warranty or repair work. It just doesn't get any better than that.

The new Fin-Nor spinning reel is built like a small tank. It has aluminum housing, brass gears, a huge cork drag system, and surprisingly few moving parts. It's a nuts-and-bolts reel that gets the job done day in and day out. At the shop that I work in part-time, we see very few Quantums and Fin-Nors come back with problems or for service work. To me, that speaks volumes.

A selection of Quantum, Fin-Nor, and Van Staal spinning reels, which are now among the most popular brands for both surf casting and boat fishing.

Quantum has introduced its version of the baitrunner series of spinning reels. These reels allow spin fishermen to fish their reels in free spool, like anglers that use casting reels. You engage the free-spool lever after casting. When you get a strike, turn the handle to re-engage the reel and drag.

Rods

The wide range of rods available today run the gamut of quality and price, but there are lots of good, inexpensive rods for anglers to choose from. Many of the rods coming in from overseas have the look and feel of custom-built sticks. It's getting harder and harder to recommend a $200 rod when a $75 rod will do the same job.

I prefer a rod that is made from some sort of composite, such as S-Glass or E-Glass, in conjunction with graphite. All-graphite rods are much too stiff, much too brittle, and break all too easily when nicked or scratched. Just look at how many professional bass anglers are going back to using

Learn to flip the bail with your hand instead of turning the reel's handle to eliminate a quarter-turn of the spool that can twist your line after a lot of casts. It also gives you more control of your lure while casting.

Rods are available in a wide range of lengths and actions. I like a 7-foot, medium-heavy action rod (either casting or spinning) for most of my fishing.

pure fiberglass for some specific applications. The composite blanks are much tougher and offer a lot more forgiveness when a big fish tries to free himself or makes strong lunges when hooked.

From observing literally thousands of anglers fishing not only on my boat but other charter boats as well, I've found that a stiff rod can be a serious drawback if you aren't used to using one. Most anglers are tempted to try and crank the fish in as fast as possible, which is a natural reaction when you realize that you have a good fish. However, trying to crank a big fish in with a rod that doesn't have much bend in it can cause the hook to tear a hole in the fish's mouth. A rod with a light tip and some forgiveness bends when the fish lunges and pulls against your line and will cut down on the number of fish you lose because the hook pulled out.

When fishing soft plastics, you will need three types of rods: light, medium, and heavy action. Unfortunately, no one particular rod or action will be able to cover the wide range of weights and sizes of plastic

Muskie rods were developed for fish that grow to enormous proportions, so they are well suited for targeting big stripers. They are light in weight and very powerful.

baits. Big, heavy plastics require a heavy stick to get a good hook-set. Smaller plastics require a lighter, more flexible stick to work them correctly.

For fishing live bait, I like rods that are made for muskie fishing. Most of these rods are built from some sort of composite material. They are lightweight, have plenty of backbone in the lower portion of the blank, and are crafted with big fish in mind. I like the Quantum Affinity Swimbait rod. At 7 feet 9 inches, it's a heavy-duty rod built for the giant swimbaits that have become popular out west. Some of these new baits weigh 6 to 8 ounces and are 12 to 14 inches long, so the rod is more than capable of handling big saltwater lures and baits.

If you fish from a boat, a rod of 7 or 7½ feet is a better choice than a shorter rod. The longer rod gives you more control over the fish. Not only do you have better leverage with a longer rod, it also gives you the reach to lead the fish around the engine or transom when it is close or dives under the boat.

The old Penn Z-Series spinning reels are regarded as one of the best spinning reels ever made for fishing live eels because of their low gear ratio. Van Staal is one of the few companies I know of that is still making a spinning reel with a 4:1 gear ratio. That's why so many anglers prefer casting reels for fishing eels.

These surf rods range in size from 9 to 11 feet and are made of fiberglass, graphite, and composite material. You can choose either spinning or casting models. Many anglers prefer the composite rods for surf casting because they will take a lot more abuse than pure-graphite models. *Ocean State Tackle photo*

Line

After working in a tackle shop, I've learned that fishermen have very strong opinions on what is a good line and what isn't. Guys who have fished for a long time have especially strong preferences for one particular brand over another. Brand loyalty is so strong, in fact, I'm not going to try and talk anyone into anything. It would likely be a waste of time.

I happen to like Sufix and Ande monofilament. They are strong, limp, and extremely abrasion resistant. I also like Sufix and Ande braided line. If you are fishing where there are a lot of rocks, I'd go

Changing your line and keeping it fresh is one of the most inexpensive things you can do to ensure you land big fish.

I like to use Sufix and Ande monofilament, though there are many great brands on the market. Fluorocarbon is a good choice when fishing around rocks. *Ocean State Tackle photo*

with the mono over the braided. Braided line is easily cut on sharp rocks. Over sand or in open water, braided line is fine. Whatever your brand preferences, buy the best line that you can afford, and change it often. A friend of mine used to buy nothing but the cheap line sold in discount stores, the kind that costs $1.99 for 250 yards. He never had a problem with his line breaking, but he would change the line religiously every three or four trips. That's the key—changing your line often, regardless of the type or the cost. It is, after all, your one and only connection to the fish and also one of the cheapest items of fishing tackle.

When fishing in rocky areas, typical of striper coastlines, braided line is the worst option. When braid comes in contact with sharp rocks, reefs, or coral, it breaks like sewing thread. And a big bass, once hooked, is almost always going to head for the biggest rock it can find.

Other Gear

Although there is an almost unlimited amount of tackle out there, much of it unnecessary, here are some additional items that I have found useful.

Snap Swivels

Try to keep the use of terminal gear to a minimum, as it is just one more thing that can fail when a big fish is on. Having said that, a good swivel helps prevent line twist, especially when using soft-plastic baits like Slug-Gos. A quality crane swivel or ball-bearing swivel is the best choice. The Spro in-line swivel is great when you are using live bait or trolling. Its narrow shape allows it to go through most guides. They are also very strong—a small one has a breaking point of 100 pounds or more.

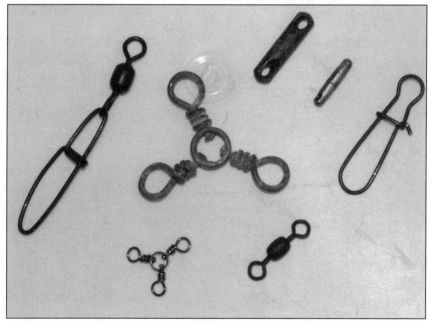

Having various types of swivels available and ready to use will make changing lures, adding lures or weights, and other necessary jobs a lot easier. Make sure to have snap swivels, trolling swivels, and three-way swivels in your gear bag.

Hook-Resistant Gloves

The best gloves that I've found are Lindy's Fishing Gloves from Lindy's Tackle Company. These gloves were originally designed for paramedics and emergency-response personnel on ambulance and rescue units. They provide the ultimate in protection from hooks, spines, gills, sharp knives, and any other sharp objects. More than once they have saved me from a trip to the hospital to have a hook removed. Putting these gloves on each and every time I go to reach for a fish to unhook him or bring him into the boat has become second nature. Going to the hospital to have a hook removed from your hand or other body part is not a nice experience.

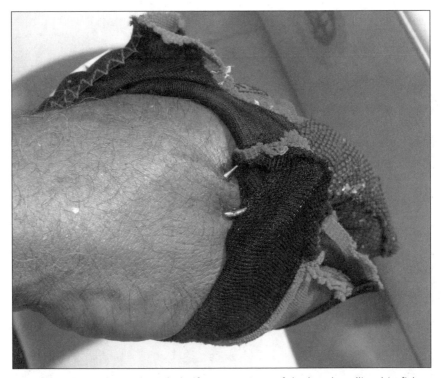

Sometimes even gloves don't help if you aren't careful when handling big fish. This hook just missed the protective layer of the glove and went into my hand. That's when having a good set of cutting pliers on board is a necessity so you can at least remove the hook from the lure, fly, or fish.

Nets, Lip Grips, Gaffs

To increase your chances of boating that monster, you should also carry a big net and a Boga Grip. The Boga Grip that goes to 60 pounds is obviously better than the 30-pound model, if you target big stripers. Only once has the 60-pound scale not been enough to weigh a fish on my boat. When it comes to nets, the Frabill brand has been the best I have found. It's the only net that hasn't bent on me after repeatedly boating big fish.

Not many people use gaffs any more, but there may be times when having one is useful. I don't usually gaff fish anymore and prefer to use a net instead, especially if the fish is going to be released alive. In fact, the last fish I gaffed was Billy Nolan's 60-pounder as I didn't want to chance missing it with the net or not having it fit in the net. Gaffs are also useful for retrieving lost hats, pot lines that get caught in the motor's prop, and other unexpected duties. They are cheap enough to have one along with you in the boat, even if you never use it.

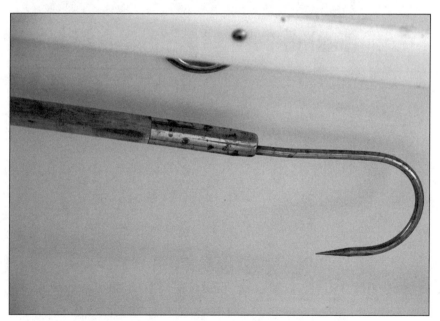

I carry a gaff on board for many purposes, but rarely use it. I did use it, however, for Bill Nolan's 60-pounder that is on the cover of this book.

Cutting Pliers

You should also have a good set of cutting pliers with you that are sharp and powerful enough to cut through the heavy wire of a #3/0 to #6/0 single hook. I can't tell you how many times I've had to cut hooks off a lure that was attached to an angler as well as the fish. This is one situation that is not only dangerous but painful as well. If no one is around to help you out, you could have a big problem on your hands. Each year I go to a hardware store and buy a pair of heavy duty cutting pliers that are capable of cutting the heavy wire of big trebles or single hooks. Most fishing pliers struggle with heavy hook wire. Any brand will do as long as they have big jaws, a good grip, and lots of leverage. Usually the pliers don't last much longer than a year since they are exposed to salt water.

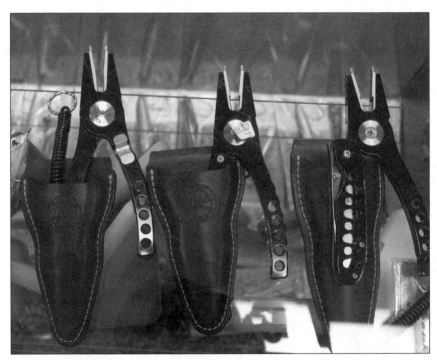

A good set of cutting pliers is essential for cutting lines, leaders, unhooking fish, and cutting hooks out of flesh. They are available in a wide range of prices and styles. *River and Riptide Anglers photo*

Scent

Sometimes using some sort of scent on your lure or flies (I know this is frowned upon by the purists) will get you more hits. Scents work especially well in dirty or roiled water, such as after a storm or in areas where there is a lot of runoff from rivers or streams. By adding scent, you increase the chances of the fish finding your lure or fly. The most effective scents remove not only foul smells but your scent as well. I've used all types and brands and they are all good. I do like Smelly Jelly, though, which is a Vaseline-type paste that stays on well once you apply it, saving you from wasting time having to continually reapply it. Other scents I've found effective are Yum, Lunker Sauce, Mustad Ultrabite, and Atlas Mike's gels.

Scents help fish find your lure or fly and work especially well in dirty water.

First-Aid Kit

Although a first-aid kit is not considered a tackle item, it should be. A good kit should be part of any angler's gear and kept either in the boat or the truck. Accidents happen all the time when fishing, and it's best to be prepared. I also carry bottles of hydrogen peroxide and rubbing alcohol to clean and disinfect any minor cuts. Many infections can turn serious quickly. I know of two people who've been hospitalized for lengthy stays from small cuts or scratches. Clean out those cuts and scratches immediately.

This young angler holds on for dear life as a big bass strips line from his light baitcasting outfit. Sometimes a big fish comes along and you haven't got the rod to control him. To land such a fish takes patience, time, and luck.

CHAPTER 14

ELECTRONICS

Q UALITY ELECTRONIC UNITS play a vital role in shallow-water fishing. The fish finder is the most widely used piece of electronic equipment in fishing today, available with a wide range of features and in a wide range of prices. Whether you fish from small craft such as canoes or kayaks or a larger V hull, you can find a model for your needs. A good electronics unit is not only a necessity for finding areas that hold fish, it also adds a measure of safety when you move from one area to the next. Knowing the water depth and the location of big boulders, rock piles, and other bottom obstructions is critical when you are on the water.

High quality units have a map feature that shows you what types of bottom structure exist below you that you can use in combination with the GPS, which enables you to go back to the same fish-holding areas that you spotted on your fish finder by simply following the map of where you have been. On a Lowrance unit, you can also mark these features by hitting the waypoint button feature twice and it will remember that position for you automatically.

Fish-finding units have come a long way since I first owned one. My

Our Triton 23-foot center console with a 225 horsepower E-Tec fuel-efficient outboard and outfitted with all the latest electronics has made all the difference in helping us find fish and get to where we need to be quickly and safely.

first unit was a Raytheon paper machine that recorded data sideways. By today's standards, it seems like a Buck Rogers toy compared to the Star Wars units now available. Those older machines ate paper rolls at a phenomenal rate, as well as making a lot of noise and dust as they burned marks on the paper. However, they did force you to pay close attention to the readings and what they were trying to tell you. Now, many years later, I believe I was fortunate to have begun with a unit like that, as it taught me how to read and interpret information.

It takes a long time to learn what a unit is showing you on the screen, and even longer to interpret it correctly. As always, there is room for improvement, and like fishing itself, you never get to know it all. This was driven home to me hard when I had the opportunity to film the TV show *One More Cast* with BASS pro Shaw Grigsby, the fourth all-time money winner on the professional bass circuit.

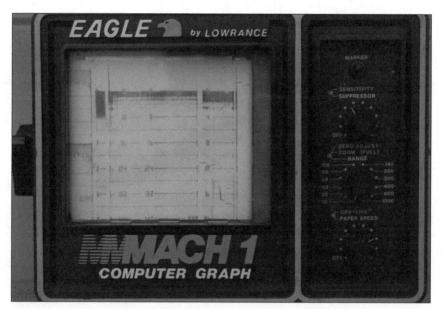

This old Eagle paper machine worked well for years before being replaced by new technology. These machines were loud, dusty, and used an awful lot of expensive paper, but they were extremely accurate.

At the time of our filming, I had about thirty-five-years experience using all different styles and brands of electronic fish finders. After spending four days fishing with Shaw, I quickly found out how little I knew and how much more I had to learn. We were using a state-of-the-art Lowrance LCX-104 color machine, the same unit I have on my boat. When Shaw finished showing me things on this unit I had no idea even existed, I was completely flabbergasted, as well as having to swallow a big piece of humble pie. The point is that if you own any type of high-quality electronic unit, it will most likely provide you with information that you never thought possible. Read your owner's manual from cover to cover, and then read it over again.

The Lowrance LCX-104 has a massive 15½-inch color screen, the same as used in laptop computers. It has mapping, fish-finding, and radar capability all in one unit. Bottom readings are shown in great detail, and you won't see anything that really isn't there. The older

Lowrance fish-finder unit showing big fish next to a school of bait that is moving toward shallow water. Lowrance is making one of the best fish-finding units on the market today. Its quality is second to none and as close to commercial grade as the average consumer can get.

Lowrance X-15 paper machines, and then the LMS units that evolved into detailed digital units, were used by countless agencies for search-and-rescue missions. Known for their extreme accuracy and detailed picture display of the bottom, Lowrance has gained an impeccable reputation among both freshwater and saltwater fishermen.

Since the initial introduction of sonar fish finders some sixty years ago, the basic concept is still pretty much the same. Fish finders operate by sending a sound wave through the water and measuring the time it takes for the wave to return from either the bottom or a target in between. All units consist of two parts: a transmitter/receiver and a transducer positioned on the boat's hull.

Transducers

Transducers help you see the bottom and whatever is swimming between it and your boat. A transducer is similar to a radio antenna. It changes electrical waves into sound waves and then turns the returning sound waves back into electrical energy so that the transmitter/receiver can interpret them. Sound travels through the water at 4,800 feet per second and in a consistent manner. It's therefore possible to calculate the time of their journey and determine the distance they have traveled.

The lower the frequency of the sound wave, the farther it will travel. Transducers come in two frequencies: 50 kHz and 200 kHz. The 50 kHz is good for probing water up to and over 1,000 feet in depth, and therefore is the choice for deep-water fishing. The 200 kHz is good for water up to 350 feet, and as most inshore fishing is done in water much shallower than this, such a model will suffice. However, some of the newer, higher-priced units have both frequencies built into their transducers.

The very best placement of a transducer is inside the hull so the sound wave is shot through the hull. This placement allows high-speed readings (up to about 40 miles per hour) without any distortion or loss of bottom readings. The second best placement is a through-the-hull installation, which involves cutting a hole in the bottom of your boat and plugging it with the transducer. Maybe it's me, but I've never felt that cutting a hole in the bottom of my boat was a good idea. However, a lot of anglers install them this way.

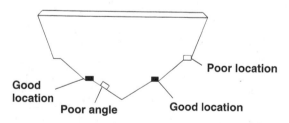

This diagram shows the proper placement of a transducer on the back of your boat. Some like to place it inside the hull and epoxy it in place, while others like to go through the hull for installation. I have a problem with cutting a hole in the bottom of my boat and prefer one of the first two methods when installing a transducer. *Illustration courtesy of Lowrance*

The third place to mount the transducer is by bolting it on the outside of the transom. You'll need to pay close attention to the manufacturer's directions about where to place it, though, because if you select the wrong position, the unit will display a lot of interference, which translates into false readings and nonfactual data, especially when the boat is moving.

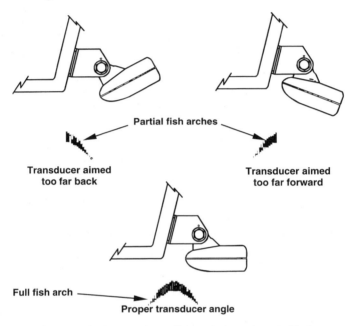

Partial fish arches

Transducer aimed too far back

Transducer aimed too far forward

Full fish arch

Proper transducer angle

If your unit is showing the inverted "v" fish arch then there is likely something wrong with the placement of your transducer. It's either pointing up to high or down too low to pick up the correct fish signals.

Transducer alignment. The most critical aspect of correct fish-finder readings is the proper placement and alignment of the transducer with the bottom of the boat. Your owner's manual will show you exactly where and how to do this. *Illustrations courtesy of Lowrance*

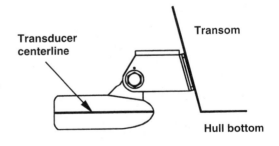

Transom

Transducer centerline

Hull bottom

Fish-Finder Features

The modern sonar unit has improved dramatically in its ability to interpret raw data and soundings and translate them into a finished product. A stand-alone depth finder is the simplest of all the units. It only has to calculate the depth of the water and then display that reading. Fish finders operate at a much higher level. They identify targets, as well as their distance from the surface and location relative to the boat, and show them onscreen.

Most units today are built inside waterproof housings, which is a big improvement over their predecessors. They have advanced microprocessor technology and screens that are readable in direct sunlight. (In the old days, units in open boats required a sun screen during the day.) The Lowrance 104 is totally viewable during bright sunshine, and also has a nighttime viewing feature—a black background with bright green symbols that makes the screen viewable from anywhere in the boat.

Take trips on the water in which you don't fish but simply experiment with your fish finder and learn what it is showing you.

Today's units are available in monochrome as well as color. Color units show the intensity of a signal in various shades of color so you can determine its strength. Once you become familiar with these color readings, you can then determine the hardness or softness of the bottom, find schools of baitfish, and even identify what types of fish are passing beneath your boat.

Most of the better units also offer some combination of bottom lock, bottom zoom, and white-line capability. Lowrance offers Bottom Track, which enables the unit to keep track of the bottom and holds its position during boat movement, keeping the unit from jumping in and out of its bottom range. Quite a few units have standard bottom zoom in 2X to 4X magnification. This helps you find small, subtle bottom changes and bottom-holding fish.

The white line feature presents the bottom as a line of varying thickness, depending on how hard or how soft the bottom is. A thin line depicts a very hard bottom of rock or a ledge, while a broader line indicates

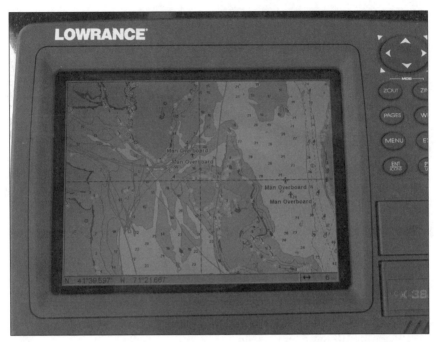

Here is a chart recorder reading from our Lowrance LX-26 machine. The maps in GPS units today are simply amazing and very accurate, and they allow you to find all types of bottom structure and new areas to fish—once you learn how to read them.

a soft mud or sand bottom. The technology is based on how the bottom reflects sound waves. A hard bottom does not allow sound to travel through it, so the time the signal takes to return is much less. A soft bottom absorbs sound, so the sound waves go deeper, producing a thicker line on the viewing screen.

If the unit has fish symbols, turn that feature off and use the "arc" symbols for better readings.

The bottom line to any unit, no matter how expensive or inexpensive, is knowing how to use it, and that takes time on the water and years of trial-and-error. There really isn't any magic unit on the market that you can turn on and instantly find fish.

GPS/Chart Plotters

GPS has revolutionized marine charting and positioning accuracy. It has even moved beyond the expectations of the most devout Loran-C users, although many of the older guys still like their units.

Today's technology has certainly reduced the number of factors that you need to consider when buying one of these units. Almost all manufacturers are using the Wide Area Augmentation System (WAAS) to

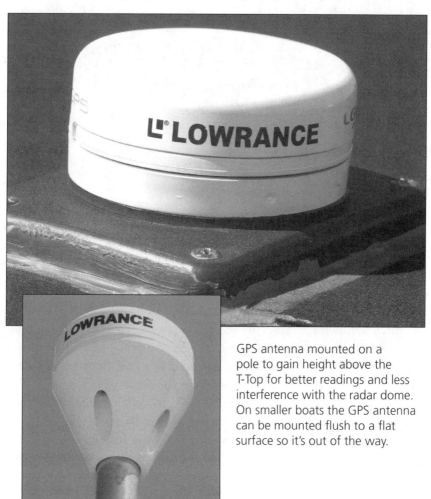

GPS antenna mounted on a pole to gain height above the T-Top for better readings and less interference with the radar dome. On smaller boats the GPS antenna can be mounted flush to a flat surface so it's out of the way.

E V O L U T I O N   O F   G P S

The first improvement in GPS occurred when the U.S. government turned off Selective Availability (SA). With SA turned off, the typical GPS fix improved from 100 meters (328 feet) in radius to 25 meters (82 feet). The second big improvement was using a differential signal to augment GPS. The DGPS technology was developed to improve accuracy of the GPS signal that had been degraded by the SA system. DGPS depends on a land-based location receiver that receives signals from twelve different satellites, then determines the difference between those locations, calculates a correction, and transmits the corrected signal over local radio beacon frequencies.

The last big development was the introduction of WAAS, which uses two Geostationary Earth Orbit (GEO) satellites in conjunction with a network of ground reference stations. The WAAS signal corrects a number of factors that cause degradation of its signal, including GPS satellite orbit, signal delays from the atmosphere, and clock drift. WAAS is accurate to a radius of 3 meters (10 feet).

give you accuracy within 5 meters of a target. Some of the more sophisticated units, like the Lowrance 104, provide both WAAS and Differential GPS (DGPS) and switch back and forth for the most accurate positioning under all conditions.

There is absolutely no reason whatsoever to venture out on the water today without some sort of GPS system. GPS units are available as small as 2-inch x 4-inch handheld models all the way up to models you mount on a console or inside an electronics box. Some of the smaller handheld units even have a database and map capability that can be downloaded from CD-ROMs. These units are good for those who like to fly fish beaches, rivers, and estuaries at night. You can mark locations where you have found fish and return to them even when it's pitch black.

As mentioned above, color-screen technology has improved to the point where you can view these detailed maps in direct sunlight. The most popular maps are C-Map and Navionics. I've used both types, and I don't see all that much difference, although I did settle on the Navionics version for my unit.

If you're serious about catching big stripers on a fairly regular basis, then a quality electronic unit is a must. The cheap units only show the water depth and those silly fish symbols on the display screen. They were designed more for catching fishermen than catching fish. First, they have little or no power to probe the water efficiently. Second, their electronic filtering system is set so low that virtually anything beneath the boat can set off those useless fish symbols. This is easily seen when you go over a perfectly flat, unobstructed bottom and fish symbols magically appear all over the screen from top to bottom. You're not going to find many striped bass or any gamefish holding over a perfectly flat bottom, especially the big ones. Yet many anglers view the screen as telling them the truth and believe the area is loaded with fish, wasting a lot of valuable time.

CHAPTER 15

KAYAKS

KAYAKS ALLOW ANGLERS TO FISH QUIETLY and efficiently in only inches of water. Their low profile, lightness in weight, and ease of paddling make them the perfect crafts for fishing in shallow water. Kayaks allow you to catch big fish in shallow water on a consistent basis if you put in the time and the effort.

Because you are so low, fishing from them—fly fishing, especially—takes a bit of extra practice. But long casts aren't all that critical since you can get very close to the structure you want to fish. You are low to the water and almost silent and that helps offset the need for long casts. I have, however, seen some fly casters who are pretty good at getting their line out there, even while sitting low to the water.

This part of the sport is evolving and changing at a rapid pace, and a lot of guys out there know and understand an awful lot more about this area of the sport than I do or ever will know. I include this chapter in my book simply because kayak fishing has become so popular and is currently one of the fastest growing segments of the sport. If you are interested in fishing from a kayak, then I encourage you to investigate it further and learn more about it from those who are experts in the field.

Trolling

Kayakers are now slow-trolling tube-and-worm combos in shallow water and racking up some impressive catches. Tube-and-worm rigs look like they would only scare fish, but they have been around for some time and can be very effective. As the name implies, the rig consists of two parts: the tube and the worm. The tube portion is simply an 18-inch piece of surgical tubing (you can use longer or shorter, depending on the purpose) that's been dyed red, amber, black, or another color. The hook is attached to a piece of flexible wire run through the tube. You can also add a stinger hook to the main hook. Some tubes come with spinners, beads, and all sorts of other stuff, but the best tubes are the plain ones.

Usually a live sea worm is added to the hook for scent and the whole thing is then let out and slowly trolled behind the boat over any type

This big bass was caught by trolling a tube-and-worm rig in just a few feet of water. Kayaks allow anglers to go where no one else can. *Brad Speck photo*

Trolling a tube-and-worm rig from a kayak is an effective way to catch large bass in shallow water.

of structure. The tube and worm slowly spin in a corkscrew motion as you troll the rig so it is important to use a good ball-bearing swivel between your main line, the leader, and the tube so your line doesn't twist. One of the more popular tubing systems is the T-Man tube. It allows you to use various weights of egg sinkers to adjust the depth for deep water or strong currents.

Big tube-and-worm rigs are extremely effective on big stripers when trolled on either leadcore or wire line, but kayakers are trolling where a normal boat would have difficulty—in water less than 5 feet deep. They can go slow, so if they do encounter a rock or hazard, it's usually not serious. Kayak anglers are catching more and larger fish as they learn how to refine this old technique. Fish are now being taken on a regular basis reaching into the 30-pound class and higher by fishermen who are plying the waters in their small craft. It's becoming an extremely effective method for taking monster shallow-water stripers during the day as well as the night.

Safety

Don't paddle across the main traffic lane on a bay or river when there is a 3-foot wind chop. It's almost impossible to see you and downright dangerous to try and traverse such areas during peak boating times, particularly weekends. Pick a bright boat color that can easily be seen when fishing in big water. Orange, yellow, or red is more visible than blue or green. Some kayakers I know have their boats outfitted with pennants and orange flags so they are visible under most weather and water conditions. Pay particular attention to the weather. Bouncing up and down in 3- to 4-foot seas and getting lost in the trough of a wave can have serious consequences. Yes, there are power boaters out there that are a danger to themselves as well as others on the water. But they are usually easy to spot.

I was once up in the tower of a friend's 45-foot Hatteras, sitting at idle, watching the Jamestown Bridge being blown up by the Army

Light, life jackets, and waterproof clothing are necessary for safe fishing at night in a kayak.

Corp of Engineers. I suddenly heard a voice call out, "Good morning. Have they blown the bridge up yet?" I turned around and looked down to see three kayakers directly behind the transom of the boat. I asked them if they had some sort of death wish, being so close. They seemed to have no idea of what I was talking about or why I was asking them such a question. I told them that if the captain didn't see them and turned the boat to port or starboard, or worse yet, backed up, we'd run them over. A boat of that size just doesn't move out of the way. This is only one incident among many from my years on the water. Use common sense while on the water.

Captain Jerry Sparks points out that you should also wear a bright PFD. If you should go in the water and become immobile or unconscious, rescuers can more easily find you if are wearing something bright that stands out. This also makes you more visible from the sky or from a great distance. That could save your life. If you choose to use one of the inflatable SOS products, then wear a bright shirt. He also

Handling big bass like this one in a kayak requires patience as well as practice. Hook a big fish like this and you are in for the ride of your life.

You can get close to blitzing fish in a kayak—right in the middle of the action.

adds that specialty packs are available that come stored in their own waterproof bags and will fit easily into one of the storage compartments on the kayak itself. The kits have signal mirrors, whistles, flares, and all the safety gear you'd need. There's even a small hand pump for bailing out water. There is really no reason not to have the proper safety equipment with you.

Because I am no kayak angler, I figured I'd get some expert advice on the topic from Capt. Jerry Sparks of Coventry, Rhode Island, who is an expert on the subject, as he not only fishes and charters out of a kayak, but he is also a manufacturer's rep.

Two happy anglers show off the rewards of fishing in shallow water with kayaks. *Photos courtesy of Hobie*

Sparks on Kayaks

Selecting a Boat

In open water, the best choice is the sit-on-top model. These boats are completely self-bailing, which means that any water that comes into the craft automatically goes out. You can also launch sit-on-tops in the surf without fear of swamping or sinking them. These boats are great for guys who fish the beach. Many times the fish are just out of reach to surf casters, and that can be frustrating. If you have a kayak with you, you can launch it and quietly approach those schools that are feeding just out of casting range. In my opinion, every surf caster should have one on his truck with him for such occasions. Launching a kayak is a pretty simple task. All you need is a clear open space at the water's edge, and you're in. This opens up a lot of fishing areas. In addition to the ease of launching, they are also very easy to transport.

Heritage's new Native Water Craft has a tunnel hull that makes it totally stable and safe when standing and casting. It is also capable of floating in just inches of water. It is available in 12-, 14-, and 16-foot models, as well as in a two-seater for fishing with a buddy.

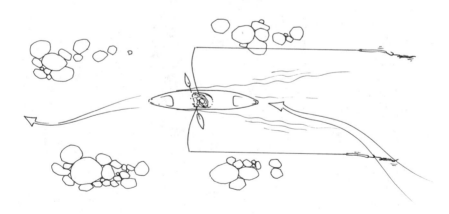

This diagram shows a typical kayak trolling pattern in shallow water. Rod holders will hold the rods out in the proper position as you paddle in and around any structure.

A completely tricked-out kayak ready for fishing with either fly rods or light tackle. There isn't anything that this small boat doesn't have in it. *Hobie photo*

The Hobie pedal-drive has a set of pedals, like a bike, that you control with your feet. They are attached to paddles beneath the boat so you can control the speed and movement of the boat hands-free while fishing. These boats have become very popular with the guys who like to drag a tube-and-worm rig around in shallow water.

Paddles

Paddles range from inexpensive models to ones costing hundreds of dollars. They are made of plastic as well as high-tech carbon fiber, which is extremely lightweight yet has superior strength. Most kayak centers have guys who do this for a living and know what they are talking about, so take their advice when purchasing a paddle.

Serious kayak anglers usually opt for the carbon-fiber paddles. Those who are new to the sport normally choose the less inexpensive models until they see if they like them or not. In some cases, depending

Captain Jerry Sparks with a nice striper taken in the shallow waters of a back bay. Capt. Sparks has built a guide service around fishing out of kayaks and is considered an expert in their use and rigging for fishing.

on the size and type that you choose, it can be a mistake to go with the low-end paddles. My best advice is to buy the best paddle that you can afford. In the long run it will pay off in less work, less frustration, and a lot more enjoyment on the water.

I invented a paddle with a built-in fish scale called the Angler. I came up with the concept and the company liked it, so it went into production and is now available to everyone. The company is Bendy's Branches, and they are making top-quality kayak paddles. Their line includes the Slice and the Breeze models. One is graphite and the other has a carbon-fiber blade.

Some companies have stake-out push-poles that have a paddle on one end and a stake-out tip on the other. Once you find an area to fish or a hot bite, you can stake out your boat without having to drop an anchor to hold yourself in position while you fish. It gives an angler a bit of an edge when fishing in skinny water.

Kayaks today can be outfitted with GPS units, sonar, marine radios, rod holders for trolling, and a lot more. It's amazing what you can attach to one. There are all sorts of add-ons that are capable of holding all the electronics you could possibly want to put on a boat. They've really evolved into high-tech fishing machines.

PrecisionPak has a complete line of kayak accessories. Their YakPak will hold all your lure boxes, and it has rod holders, dry storage compartments, map compartments, and two models with a self-contained live well system as well as a built-in tackle system. For those who like to keep an occasional fish or two, there are fish bags that can be hung over the side of the boat to keep the fish fresh until you are done fishing.

Then there is clothing. Emerson Research from Pennsylvania has dry tops as well as dry pants for kayakers, and PrecisionPak offers three styles of dry tops for surf casting and kayaking. This is one of the crossover products that I have seen thus far. The Gator Company offers neoprene waterproof socks, as well as other clothing items. Then there is specialized footwear. MTI manufactures life jackets for anglers, and Keen Footwear offers waterproof booties, sandals, high ankle boots, and quick-drying shoes.

Pelagic Outdoor Wear sells an AquaSkin shirt. You can actually pour water on it and it beads up and rolls right off. When I do my

If you are lucky enough to hook a bass this big, you can be sure he'll take you on a Nantucket sleigh ride. Big bass are strong and powerful creatures, especially when hooked in shallow water. *Mike Laptew photo*

seminars and demonstrations at shows, I'm usually in a pool of water. I bring a cup with me and demonstrate how waterproof this shirt actually is. When the audience sees the results of me pouring water all over myself, they all immediately want to know where they can buy that shirt. The best part is this shirt is not just for kayakers but anyone who fishes.

Many kayakers use specialized rack systems to put on your car or truck, and also kayak-specific trailers. Thule's Hullavator comes down alongside of the vehicle for easy loading and unloading. The accessories attach easily and quickly, so putting them on or taking them off doesn't require a lot of time. Specialized kayak trailers are also available.

CHAPTER 16

WEATHER

NATURE HAS HONED the senses of striped bass to razor sharp proportions to help them survive in an extremely hostile environment. Striped bass are one of nature's top predators in the ocean when it comes to understanding and using the changes in weather patterns to their advantage. Their senses tell them when changes are coming as well as triggering them to either feed, rest, or hide. If there is a creature on earth who actually understands the weather, then it has to be the striper, even with a pea-sized brain and lack of satellites or computer models.

In our world, as well as the fish's world, the weather can change hourly, as well as daily. It may take some time, but the bass will eventually adjust to those changes and adapt their behavior. With a better understanding of weather, you can be in the right place, as well as the right time, to catch big bass.

Weather is used more often as an excuse for not catching fish than all other excuses combined—it was too hot, too cold, too windy, too rainy, and on and on. But it's easier to blame the weather than it is to admit that we don't know how to deal with the conditions. Weather not

Capt. John Luchka with a huge striper caught just before a storm in New York. *Captain John Luchka photo*

only affects how, when, and where you fish, it will also determine just how often fish will feed and be active. It is also one of the least written about topics in angling, probably because it is so complicated. And besides, who really understands the weather to begin with? Certainly not those who forecast it on the evening news, for if we had to depend on them, we'd all be in trouble. I am by no means a trained meteorologist, but experience has taught me many lessons when dealing with the weather. The first of which is there is absolutely nothing we can do about it or anything we can do to control its effects. Second, if you ignore it, you may pay with your life.

> Excellent fishing will occur just before a frontal system moves into an area after a period of stable weather.

Water Temperature

About five years ago I started to delve into the winter fishery in our local rivers. What I've seen has changed my opinion about almost anything to do with water temperature and how it affects fish and fishing. On one outing, I was fishing with my long-time friend Mike McElroy. We went to a river in lower Massachusetts on January 5, 2003. The air temperature was 38 degrees, it was cloudy, and snow was forecast for the late morning. We launched his tin boat and headed upriver. When we arrived at one of Mike's spots, we circled the water twenty or thirty times to break the ice on the surface of the river. In this area we caught six school bass of about 22-inches. He then decided to head upriver to fish a flat where the water was only four to five feet deep. He put on a 6-inch white Slug-Go, made a cast, and immediately caught a fish. For the next two hours we landed fish after fish, losing count somewhere around seventy bass. Oh, did I mention that it began to snow about twenty minutes after we arrived? On this particular river there is no power plant or anything else to warm the water artificially. It's a simple tidal river, that's all.

Connecticut's Thames River is now world famous for its winter striper fishing. Capt. Al Anderson, who runs charters there in the middle of winter, has caught thousands of stripers for his clients and is credited with tagging and releasing more than 50,000 striped bass for the American Littoral Society. He does this in freezing temperatures, with ice on the water, sometimes in deep water and sometimes in the shallows. On many mornings, he also breaks ice to reach open water.

I've also had some great days when the water is just below 80 degrees, which some say is too warm for bass. If there is a lot of bait, with little or no rain to lower the water's salinity in the shallows and the fish get hungry, they will eat even if the water is 80 degrees. It may not last long, but they will eat. The same is true for when the water is cold. If there is lots of bait, and the fish are there, they will eat. A contradiction? Absolutely. If I stayed home and watched TV every time I thought or believed that the water was either too cold or too hot, I'd never catch any fish. In my business I don't have the option or the luxury of staying home when conditions aren't perfect. I have to play the hand each new day deals.

Billy "Bunker" Nolan (I gave him the nickname after he caught so many big fish using live bunker) with a 50-pound bass he caught the week before he got his 60.

Low Light

Water temperature may be one of the factors affecting fishing, but it's not nearly as important as how much light there is on any given day. A simple rule of thumb is the brighter the day is, the more difficult it will be to get a big fish to eat a lure or fly. You may have noticed that bright blue skies with no clouds at all make for some of the worst fishing days of the entire year. Darker days will normally dramatically improve the bite in any given area, sometimes regardless of the water temperature.

This general principle is what makes night fishing for stripers so good. Take, for example, the darkness of a new moon. The fishing can be excellent. However, when the moon is full and bright and there is no cloud cover, fishing is often tough. Yet add some cloud cover to a full moon, and the fish can go wild. There are, of course, exceptions to this.

One puzzling phenomenon is that although the fishing is usually pretty good at dusk, after the sun sets and it begins to get darker, the fishing continually slows and comes to a standstill as the light vanishes. I've never found a logical reason for this, except the explanation that the fish need time to adjust to the diminishing light. Those who stay for a while and continue fishing through this slow period usually begin catching fish after a few hours. In some areas this lull doesn't happen at all, and the bite continues right into dark.

Low light and changing weather patterns can lead to excellent fishing. First light and last light can bring on a bite. Combine that with a changing weather pattern, and the fishing can be exceptional.

Weather Systems

As a storm begins to approach, cloud cover increases and the barometric pressure begins a slow and steady drop. At first, this can bring good fishing because of the low light and the fact that a drop in pressure usually triggers good fishing when it first occurs. But the storm soon brings wind and rain, and possibly thunder and lightning. Wind-swept rain tends to turn the fish off, especially in shallow water. Lightning, besides being dangerous to fishermen, will also cause the fish to become inactive.

As the low pressure system moves through, it will likely bring clearing skies (more light equals poor fishing), dropping temperatures, a lot of wind, and an increase in barometric pressure. Such changes brought by big fronts can make the bass disappear. If such an event occurs when you are fishing in shallow water, it usually means your fishing day is done. The only option is to move to deeper water and fish as slowly as possible.

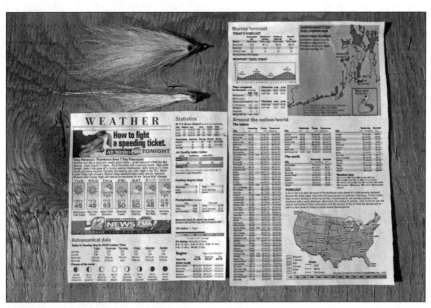

Local weather maps from the newspaper can help you track changing weather conditions. Study them to see where and in what direction weather systems will be moving.

Large stripers like bad weather, but they also like stable weather. When bad weather sets in for a few days, fishing can be excellent.

But when long periods of stable weather arrive, there will be good fishing ahead. Generally speaking, the more stable the weather, the better the fishing. This holds true for pleasant conditions as well as nasty conditions. Fish can adjust to a long-lasting period of bad weather, and they will eventually move and feed, usually within forty-eight hours or so after they have had time to adjust. When this type of weather system sets in, fishing can be the best of the entire season if the system combines with good tides and little wind.

Watch your local newspaper, weather channel, or your computer for the current weather maps or charts and accompanying barometric pressure predictions. One of the best instruments you can own is a barometer and humidity gauge. You can often predict the weather and good fishing with this device simply by watching the rise and fall of the barometric pressure. A drop will signal good fishing and a strong rise in pressure will slow it down for a time. During the day when snowball clouds are low against a clear blue sky, you are going to have a tough time getting any fish to bite, especially in water of less than 10

A small hand-held VHF radio is an excellent way to track changing weather patterns, forecasts, and weather conditions and is small enough to carry with you or keep in your truck.

feet or less. Much of the time these clouds are moving quickly across the sky and will indicate that this will, in all likely hood not be a good day for big bass.

The wind has a big effect on sea conditions and the height of the waves. When the wind blows against a strong tide, such as a moon tide, and you are inside a bay or big river system, the wave action will be much higher than normal and usually higher than what is being forecast for that day. Wind will also push more water into a river or bay when it's blowing in the same direction as the tide is moving. When the wind blows against a tide, the water will take longer to drop; when it blows with the tide, the water will fall faster than normal. These factors can alter the times of high and low tides and need to be considered when fishing.

The significant element in wind direction and weather change is duration. The longer that particular condition exists, the higher the probability that the fishing will dramatically improve. The worst-case scenario is when the wind and weather patterns change every twenty-four to forty-eight hours. Under those circumstances, the fishing will likely stink. However, in my journals, I have numerous entries where a long-lasting low-pressure system came in and stayed for a week or more. By the third day, the fishing was great and remained so until it cleared. When the clearing took place, which would normally mean ideal conditions, the fishing ended abruptly.

One thing that continually amazes me, no matter how long or how much I fish, is how things can turn on and off in seconds. I guess it's one of nature's mysteries that we'll never solve.

Bill Nolan took this nice fish just before a low-pressure system arrived in the morning. Fishing low-pressure systems just before they arrive can provide some of the year's best fishing.

When the wind and tide are against each other, big waves form. This isn't a good time to be on the water.

Clouds

Clouds form when water vapor rises in invisible waves, cools, and becomes visible. When you are on the water, you should be watching the sky throughout the day. Clouds can help determine what types of weather systems are approaching.

Cloud types are grouped according to altitude. The highest-altitude clouds are cirrus ("mares' tails"). When isolated, cirrus clouds indicate stable weather, although masses of them can signal the approach of a storm front.

Warm days with partly cloudy skies are the best for fishing.

Middle-altitude clouds include altostratus, altocumulus, and nimbostratus. All appear as broad sheets of gray and can produce rain or snow.

Low-altitude clouds include stratocumulus, stratus, and cumulus. Stratocumulus are lumpy and layered. They usually follow a cold front and can produce rain. Stratus clouds are layered, low-lying clouds that

Bill Nolan landed this nice bass right after a rain storm passed through. Being on the water when a rain storm or front passes by can be a hair-raising experience, but once it's over, the fishing can turn on like someone threw a light switch.

Chris Megan hangs onto a big fish that ate his live pogy on a film shoot in early July. Once the fog cleared, the fish went on a feeding spree for about twenty minutes. Sometimes that's all you get.

cover a large area of the ocean and often produce drizzle. Cumulus clouds are the billowy clouds of sunny days, although they can develop into cumulonimbus clouds, vertically developed formations with a cauliflower shape and very dark undersides. These signal thunderstorms.

When a north wind blows and air and water temperatures drop sharply, fishing is going to be tough for twenty-four to forty-eight hours.

The lower the clouds are in the sky, the higher the possibility that there will be bad weather coming. When clouds are very low, black, and thick and can be seen on the horizon or close by, it's time to vacate the area and head to a safe port or harbor, as these are the most dangerous clouds of all. If you have ever been caught out on the water in a summer squall or a thunderstorm that came out of nowhere, you already know how quickly things can change.

Thunderstorms form when the sun heats and lifts the air. They normally build up over land because of the rise in afternoon air temperatures. When the sun goes down and the land cools, they tend to

This 50-pound striper came after a front passed. After a storm has moved through, big bass will once again begin to feed, especially if conditions have been horrible for a few days. Getting back out there and fishing when it's over can mean catching a fish of a lifetime.

dissipate. On the water, thunderstorms can spawn water spouts, which are miniature water tornadoes. Although they aren't all that common in many areas, they occur more often than you think. They aren't as powerful as land-based tornadoes, but they can capsize a boat quickly and cause serious injury. Yet another reason to avoid being caught in a thunderstorm is a phenomenon known as a "micro-burst," a sudden downdraft that can produce a powerful wind shift in seconds. It has even been known to bring down jetliners.

The best way to avoid serious weather is to use common sense. Keep an eye on the sky for sudden changes in cloud formations or a breeze that suddenly stops and goes dead calm. This is a tell-tale sign that serious weather is coming. When you see lightning in the distance, head for a safe port or your vehicle until it has passed by.

When cold fronts come through, fish will be active during the middle of the day until just after dark.

You can figure out how far away that storm is by counting the number of seconds from the time you see the first flash of lightning until you hear the first clap of thunder. Divide that number by five and it will give you a pretty close estimate of how far away the storm is in miles.

CHAPTER 17

WORKING WITH YOUR CAPTAIN

F INDING A GOOD GUIDE is a common topic of conversation among fishermen as well as on Internet chat sites. Of course, guides also have their own opinions on what makes a good client. One of the first things you can do to make your next charter or guided trip more successful is not to assume anything about what the day will bring. Assumptions normally get everyone in trouble sooner or later.

What Your Captain Expects from You

Although you have hired the captain, and not the other way around, the trip will be a lot more enjoyable for both of you if you take a moment to consider things from his perspective. I'm not asking for anyone's sympathy here, but you should realize that the captain's day starts long before you reach the dock and lasts a lot longer after you leave. If he's any good, he spends considerable time getting ready. Then

Arriving on time can mean the difference between fish like this or no fish at all. The window of opportunity is small on most days. When you show up late, you may have already missed that window and fishing can be tough. That is not your captain's fault.

when the day is done, there is cleaning the boat and gassing it up for the next day. Once home, he has to fix any broken equipment, change lines, tie flies, paint the house, fix the car, wash the dog, play with the kids (or grandkids, in my case) and then, just maybe, get some shut-eye before the next trip.

Be On Time

If there is one thing that bothers both guides and clients, it's being late for departure time at the dock. You should be on time, unless an un-foreseen situation arises. Many anglers who charter a trip don't seem to understand that in some areas being late may cost them the fish of a lifetime.

Be Truthful About Your Ability

When your captain, guide, or mate asks you what type of experi-ence you have with a particular type of gear, be as honest as you can with him. Even if you're not totally honest, the captain will know within minutes after you begin to fish, so what's the point of not being honest?

If you are going to be fly fishing and you aren't a really good fly caster, say so. It seems that too many anglers feel that there is some sort of disgrace associated with not being able to cast 100 feet. That is totally silly. In the first place, it usually isn't necessary to cast a fly that far. Would it help if you could? It certainly would, but it isn't neces-sary. If you do need to cast that far, you could use a spinning rod or a casting rod instead, in which case you just might catch more fish. If you can't use either of those two types of gear, at least your guide can likely teach you enough in a short time to get you through the day. Try-ing to hide the obvious just makes everyone's job harder. There is only so much that can be done in a short amount of time, so it helps to be honest from the beginning.

Learn to Reel with Both Hands

Do yourself a favor and learn to reel with both hands when you are fly fishing. Some captains have either right- or left-handed reels, but not both. Some reels can be a pain to switch over, and doing so costs

A lot of fishermen opt to catch a 41-pounder like this one instead of a boatload of little fish. You need to let your captain know beforehand, as it will affect what he does and where he goes that day. Many areas are not conducive to both numbers and large size of bass.

valuable fishing time. From the captain's perspective, the expense of keeping both types of reels is prohibitive, and it also takes up limited space on board. So, if you are going to use the guide's tackle, be prepared to reel from either side.

In regards to using either right- or left-handed reels, Lefty Kreh does a demonstration where he takes one reel of each side, lays out all the line, and then picks someone from the crowd to reel in each one. In the many years that he has done this, the person that reels in with the right-hand retrieve has always beaten the one with the left-hand version. It doesn't matter who's doing the reeling—man, woman, child, young or old—the result is always the same.

Heed the Captain's Fishing Advice

Try to go when the captain tells you the best time is. You may not like getting up at three or four in the morning, but knowing the best time is one of the reasons that you are paying him in the first place. Also, if he tells you that the particular species you are looking to catch is not available at that time and that you should target something else, then take his advice. I've had clients call in the middle of August and ask me to take them to catch keeper stripers—during the day, no less. I tell them that the only way to catch stripers at that time of year is to fish at night. They then say that they don't like night fishing. I then offer a trip for bluefish and tell them they will likely catch so many that their arms will ache. They still insist on trying for keeper bass during the day. I reply, you don't want a guide; you're looking for a magician.

Important Extras

Bring a good quality pair of sunglasses, especially if you expect to sight-cast for stripers. There are a lot of good glasses on the market today. However, with today's advanced technology, you can get the same polarizing qualities from glasses that are much less expensive than the top-name brands. Not only will good glasses help you spot more fish, whether inshore or offshore, but they will also protect your eyes from the bright sun and ultraviolet rays.

Wear shoes that don't have black soles or at least ones that don't leave those black scuff marks on the deck. There is nothing worse than trying to clean up those scuff marks at the end of the day. It will help keep your captain happy all day long knowing that he doesn't have to be on his knees for two hours scrubbing.

Definitely bring rain gear. No matter how good you think the weather will be, bring it. During the spring it will keep the cold spray off your dry clothes, and if the weather turns bad—and it does sometimes, very quickly—it will keep you dry. Rain gear also aids in cutting the wind, should it pick up during your trip, and it will also cut the wind as you are running.

Your Gear or the Captain's?

Most good captains will have good equipment. If the captain's is better than yours, then by all means use it. We have brand new Quantum and Fin-Nor casting and spinning reels and Thomas & Thomas fly gear on board all the time. It's there for our clients to use if they wish to. Leave your rod tubes and cases in your car or truck. Space on a boat is limited.

Stay Focused

Trying to do too many things in one day is also not a good idea for either you or your guide. I get requests all the time to baitfish as well as to fly fish on the same day. Or one guy will want to fly fish and one spin fish, which on some days is perfectly fine but on many others just doesn't work, especially if the fly caster isn't up to speed on his casting skills.

Some anglers want to learn as well as catch a boatload of fish, all in a four- to six-hour trip. This usually results in not getting either accomplished. Decide first on what's going to be the most important thing for you to have a successful day, and then do that one particular thing. Your money will be well spent in this endeavor and you can always come back and catch your fill of fish. Both you and the guide will get along much better, and your experience will be a memorable one.

The Captain's Word is Law

After being in business for more than eighteen years, it still amazes me how many guys can't accept the fact that on the water, the captain's word is law. He is not acting out a movie part or trying to re-create Captain Bligh, he is simply following current United States Coast Guard regulations and maritime law. Your own personal comfort and safety are his primary responsibility. Catching a boatload of fish actually comes in at number two. It will likely be the only time that you will ever pay someone to give you orders, but that's how it works. Always remember that you are not only paying him to help you catch fish, but also to use his good judgment and experience on the water should a dangerous situation arise.

What You Should Expect from Your Captain

As a paying client, you have the right to expect both professionalism and expertise from your captain. It is his responsibility to not only put you over fish, but to treat you respectfully and keep you safe.

Don't Take Abuse

One thing that you can insist on is not taking any abuse from your guide. I get clients all the time who make mistakes, like blowing a cast or losing a nice fish. Most times they stop, stare at me, and wait for a barrage of vulgarities to come flying out of my mouth. Most are shocked when it doesn't happen. Fishing is about having fun and enjoying the day with friends and the time that you spend on the water. Abusive comments by so-called professional guides are totally uncalled for. Your captain should treat you with respect and dignity at all times, even if he doesn't like you. You don't have to tolerate being yelled at, cursed at, or ridiculed all day long. From what I hear from some of my clients, this is a lot more common than one would like to believe.

Your captain should be pleasant, cheerful, easy to talk to, and most of all, informative. You are paying him for his knowledge and experience, as well as putting you over fish. A good guide will teach you something all day long—a new casting technique or how to improve an old one, how to fish a particular piece of water, what to look for on the water, types of lures and flies to use, and how to tie or rig them. If the fishing is slow or the day is just bad, you should still feel like you have spent a day in school or had your own private seminar once you have finished.

Ask About His License

I'm still amazed at how many clients never ask me if my license is current, if I even have one, or if I'm insured. It is your right to know the answer to those questions. Politely ask your captain for his license number. A professional will appreciate the request and will gladly give it to you or show you his certificate. There are an awful lot of guides today who are not trained, not insured, not licensed, and have little or no experience on the water. Today, if you have a pocketful of money, you can literally buy your license and go into business.

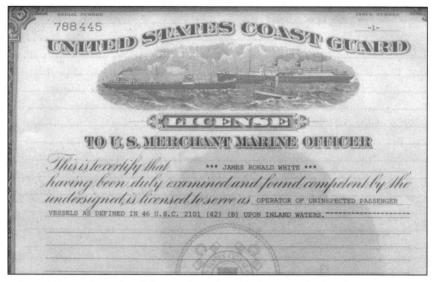

Ask to see your captain's license when you arrive. By law he is supposed to have it available and on board at all times to show anyone who asks, especially paying clients.

No Alcohol or Drugs

No professional captain should be drinking during your trip, nor should he show up drunk at the dock at sunrise. A true professional will refuse all offerings of alcohol until his job is done. First of all, your life and everyone's on board is his responsibility. Second, it is against U.S. Coast Guard regulations for the captain to be drinking or taking drugs while he is in charge of or running the boat. Once the day is complete and you have returned to the dock, he can then share a beer or two with you.

It is also within your rights to inquire if he is currently enrolled in a random drug-testing program, such as those administered by a professional association or organization, and when his last drug test was and if he passed it. I keep the results of my current tests on board to show anyone who asks for them. Again, this is covered by maritime law and by Coast Guard regulations. All legitimately licensed captains should be able to produce such documentation when asked. This is for your own safety and peace of mind.

Should a Guide Fish?

Whether a guide should fish is a touchy subject with a lot of anglers. Some believe a guide should never fish under any circumstances whatsoever. Then there are those who believe it is permissible when clients aren't up to par with their fishing skills or have seriously exaggerated their expertise.

I believe that both opinions are true to some degree; it all depends on the clients. True, you are paying your captain to show you how to fish new baits or flies, what techniques you should use, and also to put you into the best locations to catch fish. But what happens when that doesn't work? What happens when the area is loaded with fish and no one is hooking up, mainly because of inexperience? When things aren't going right and the captain knows there are fish there, it benefits everyone if he makes a few casts to see whether the fish really aren't biting on that particular day. I've watched guys fish an area with no hits or even chases, then picked up a rod with a Slug-Go or Fin-S Fish and got two or three fish to attack it in the first four feet of the retrieve.

On the water things change constantly. What worked in the beginning of the week may not necessarily work on the weekend. If your guide can't figure that out and find out what has happened from just watching you, you both lose. All the good captains that I know want their clients to be more successful than they do, as this means repeat business. I've saved many a day with sub-par clients by picking up a rod, making a few casts, and seeing for myself just what the fish were looking for on that particular day. Once that's done and the clients are catching fish, there isn't any time for me to fish. In my opinion, this is your guide doing everything in his power to make sure that you catch fish.

Check a Captain's Resume

When you call your guide or captain to book a trip or you speak with him at a show, ask him what he has accomplished. "How long have you been fishing?" is a good first question. When someone asks me that question, I'm more than happy, as well as proud, to rattle off my accomplishments. If a guide or captain can't do that or hesitates in his answer, be wary.

So how do you go about finding this expert to take you and your

Capt. Jim White leans off the side to release this 50-pounder while outdoor filmmaker Mike Laptew shoots the release. *Mike Laptew photo*

Using up-to-date, well-maintained gear with fresh line leads to landing more fish.

friends fishing? First off, the guy you want will probably have a good reputation. Ask as many people you can about him and check with local bait-and-tackle shops or fishing clubs. Can he provide references that you can speak with? You need to keep in mind, though, that not everyone will get along with or agree with everyone or everything all the time. Everyone is different. Someone you might enjoy being with, others may not. That is human nature. Finally, don't depend solely on web pages or brochures. Sure, they're useful, but there is nothing like talking to your captain personally. Almost anyone can have a fancy Web site or four-color brochure.

The quality and condition of a captain's gear is also revealing, and can help you determine whether to book another trip with him. Check and see what type of equipment he is using. Is it new or old? Is it well taken care of? Is the line fresh and the spool full, or is it old and low? Is he familiar with spinning and casting as well as fly fishing? Does he use bait on occasion? (If he does, that doesn't mean he should be drawn and quartered or put in jail.)

And finally, always be wary of the captain who says he catches big-

Running a professional guide service with new equipment, gear, boats, and motors is extremely expensive today. Keep that in mind when you charter a guide, and know that most of what you are paying him is going toward running a professional operation and not going into his pocket.

ger and more fish than anyone else, all the time. The only fish he's catching is you. No one catches fish all the time, especially big ones.

One of Those Days

Lastly, if your captain puts you onto fish and you can't catch them, that's not his fault. He also cannot control the wind and weather nor make any fish bite if they don't have a mind to. It doesn't take most people long to see if a guide is working hard or not. If he does his best to find you fish, then you've got yourself a good guide. Stick with him, as it will pay off in the long run.

APPENDIX

KNOTS

YOU ONLY NEED TO MASTER a few knots. Know how to tie four or five knots blindfolded, and you'll know all the knots you will ever need. The knots that cover most situations are the Palomar, Kreh nonslip loop, improved clinch knot, surgeon's loop and surgeon's knot, the snell knot, dropper loop, and Bimini twist. Remember that knots are the weakest link between you and the fish, and more big fish are lost from tying improper knots than almost any other reason. Tying good knots is one area of fishing that you have control over, so you should practice them to perfection.

Knot diagrams courtesy of Ande Monofilament.
Kreh nonslip loop knot by Dave Hall, courtesy of Stackpole Books.

Palomar Knot

The Palomar knot is one of the strongest knots you can use, and it is easy and quick to tie. It's one of the favorites of professional bass anglers because of this, and when you are fishing for tens of thousands of dollars the last thing you need is for your knot to slip or break. I like using this knot on jigs, regular hooks when bait fishing, and sometimes even lures as it is almost 100 percent dependable in knot strength when tied correctly.

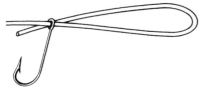

Double approximately 4 inches of line and pass the loop through the eye.

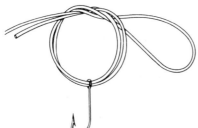

Let the hook hand loose and tie an overhand knot in the doubled line. Avoid twisting the lines and do not tighten the knot.

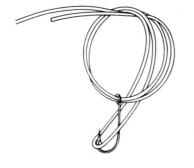

Pull loop of line far enough to pass it over hook, swivel, or lure. Make sure the loop passes completely over this attachment.

Pull both the tag end and standing line to tighten. Clip about ⅛ inch.

Kreh Nonslip Loop

An easy to tie and very strong knot for attaching flies to your leader or any other type of lure that you want to get the most action out of like on swimmers or even popping plugs. The loop allows the fly or lure to swing naturally and does not impede its action.

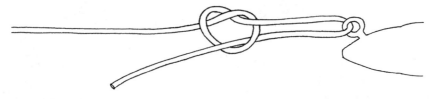

Tie an overhand knot about 4 or 5 inches above the tag end. Thread the tag end through the hook eye and pass it through the loop.

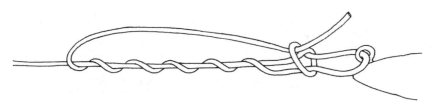

Adjust the loop size by pulling on the main line while pinching the overhand knot. Wrap the tag end around the standing line from 3 to 5 times, depending on the diameter of the monofilament. Heavier lines require fewer turns. Pass the tag end through the side of the overhand knot.

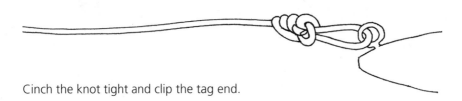

Cinch the knot tight and clip the tag end.

Improved Clinch Knot

The improved clinch is an old standard, and the knot of choice for many for tying tippet to fly or line to lure or swivel. I prefer the Palomar, but I include this knot here because it is so popular.

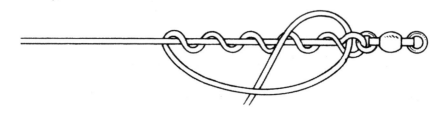

Pass the line through the eye of the hook, swivel, or lure. Double back and make five turns around the standing line. Hold coils in place; thread end of line through first loop above the eye, then through the big loop, as shown.

Hold tag end and standing line while coils are pulled up. Take care that the coils are spiraled and not lapping over each other. Slide tight against eye. Clip tag end.

Surgeon's Loop

These quick loops are necessary for attaching a leader butt to a loop on your fly line or two sections of leader with a loop-to-loop connection. You can tie a double or a triple surgeon's for extra knot strength. I've never had one fail on me yet.

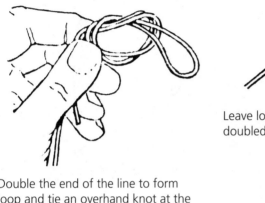

Leave loop open in knot and bring doubled line through once more.

Double the end of the line to form loop and tie an overhand knot at the base of the double line.

Hold standing line and tag end and pull loop to tighten knot. Size of the loop can be determined by pulling loose knot to desired point and holding it while knot is tightened. Clip end ⅛ inch from knot.

A proper loop-to-loop connection should form a square knot and not a girth hitch.

A properly seated loop-to-loop connection forms a square knot.

An incorrect loop-to-loop connection forms a girth hitch.

Surgeon's Knot

This knot is a fast alternative to the blood knot for tying together two pieces of line or leader material of approximately the same diameter.

Lay line and leader parallel, overlapping 6 to 8 inches.

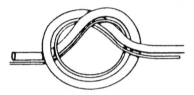

Treating the two like a single line, tie an overhand knot, pulling the entire leader through the loop.

Leaving the loop of the overhand knot open, pull both tag end of line and leader through again.

Hold both line and both ends and pull the knot tight. Clip ends.

Snelling a Hook

This knot, which is a variation on the Uni Knot, is useful for rigging eels (see page 144) and other purposes.

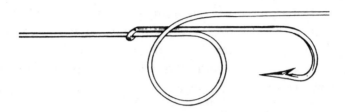

Thread line through hook eye about 6 inches. Hold line against hook shank and form a Uni Knot circle.

Make five or six turns through the loop and around line and shank. Close knot by pulling on the tag end of the line.

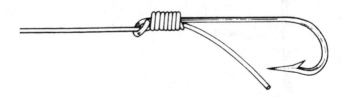

Tighten by pulling standing line in one direction and hook in the other.

Bimini Twist

I use the Bimini Twist on almost all my fly rods when rigging up for big stripers. The Bimini's double line is not only stronger, but the twists give you a cushion when a big bass slams the fly or makes a good run. It acts as a shock absorber or elastic band, and when tied correctly will stretch under pressure before it breaks. It's also a good knot to use when fishing with light tackle and light line and allows you to land bigger fish on lighter pound-test. Offshore anglers have been using this knot for decades for that one simple reason. It can make up for some human error when fighting a big fish.

Measure a little more than twice the length you'll want for the double line leader. Bring the end back to the standing line and hold them together. Rotate end of the loop 20 times (or more), putting twists in it.

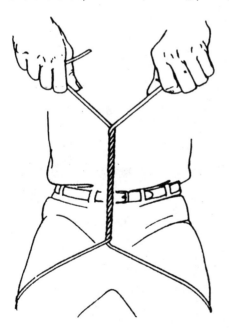

Spread loop to force twists together about 10 inches below tag end. Some anglers step through the loop to apply pressure on the twists by spreading their legs apart, others loop it over one knee, and others use two hooks screwed into a bench.

Bimini Twist (cont'd)

With the twists forced tightly together, hold the standing line in one hand with tension just slightly off the vertical position. With your other hand, move the tag end to a position at a right angle to twists. Keeping tension on the loop with knees (or other method), gradually ease tension of tag end so it will roll over the column of twists, beginning just below the upper twist.

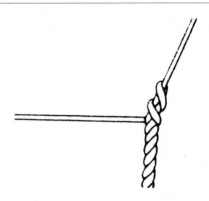

Spread legs apart slowly (or other hand if using an alternate method) to maintain pressure on loop. Steer tag end into a tight spiral coil as it continues to roll over the twisted line.

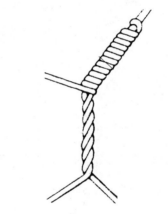

When the spiral of tag end has rolled over column of twists, continue keeping knee pressure on loop and move hand that has held standing line down to grasp knot. Place finger in crotch of line where loop joins knot to prevent slippage of last turn. Take half-hitch with tag end around nearest leg of loop and pull up tight.

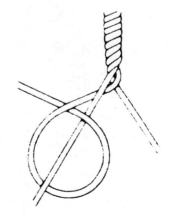

Bimini Twist (cont'd)

With half-hitch holding knot, release knee pressure but keep loop stretched out tight. Using remaining tag end, take half-hitch around both legs of loop, but do not pull tight.

Make two more turns with the tag end around both legs of the loop, winding inside the bend of line formed by the loose half-hitch and toward the main knot. Pull tag end slowly, forcing the three loops to gather in a spiral.

When loops are pulled up neatly against main knot, tighten to lock knot in place. Trim tag end about ¼ inch from knot.

Dropper Loop

The dropper loop is essential for making your own snagging rig (see page 138) or squid jigs (see page 155).

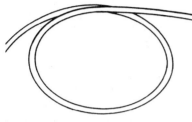

Form a loop in the line.

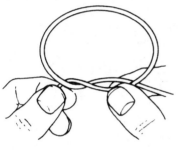

Pull one side of the loop down and begin taking turns with it around the standing line. Keep the point where the turns are made open so turns gather equally on each side.

After 8 to 10 turns, reach through the center opening and pull the remaining loop through. Keep finger in this loop so it will not spring back.

Hold loop with teeth and pull both ends of line, making turns gather on either side of loop.

Set knot by pulling lines as tightly as possible. Tightening coils will make loop stand out perpendicular to line.

INDEX

Manufacturer Contact Information

I could not write, guide, and provide my clients with the newest and latest equipment and gear on the market without my sponsor's full support and help. It's due to their generosity and faith in my ability and experience that they provide me with the best gear so our clients can have access to use it. I urge readers to support these fine outdoor companies (listed in alphabetical order) as they have supported us.

Ande Monofilament, andemonofilament.com

Bomber, bomberlures.com

Creek Chub, creekchub.com

Evinrude, evinrude.com, (847) 689-7090

Fin-Nor, fin-norfishing.com, (800) 588-9030

Heddon, heddonlures.com

Lindy, lindyfishingtackle.com, (218) 829-1714

Lowrance, navico.com

Lunker City, lunkercity.com

Matzuo America, matzuo.com, (800) 941-2029

Ocean Waves, oceanwaves.com, (800) 495-9283

Quantum, quantumfishing.com, (800) 444-5581

Rebel, rebellures.com

Ronz, ronzmfg.com, (508) 896-9185

Tattoo's Tackle, tattoostackle.com, (401) 683-9202

Thomas and Thomas, thomasandthomas.com, (413) 774-5436

Yum, yum3x.com, (479) 782-8971

ABOUT THE AUTHOR

CAPTAIN JIM WHITE has been guiding Rhode Island's salt waters for over eighteen years and is considered an expert in shallow-water bass tactics. He is a featured speaker on the seminar circuit, and his speaking engagements are always full. Jim has also received many awards for his writing and photography as well as for his tireless work for striped bass conservation. He was featured in Dick Russell's *Striper Wars: An American Fish Tale* and had the honor of testifying before both houses of Congress on striped bass issues. He has been featured on nine national television shows, as well as three cable networks for his expertise on catching big stripers in shallow water. White owns and operates White Ghost Guide Service, Ltd, along with his son, Capt. Justin White. Together they make up one of the few father-and-son fishing teams in the guide business today. White has published two other books, *New England Saltwater Fishing Guide* and *How to Fish Plastic Baits in Saltwater* and has published over 2,000 articles in national and local publications.